WTF?

How to Survive 101 of Life's
Worst F*#!-ing Situations

Gregory Bergman and Anthony W. Haddad

Avon, Massachusetts

Published by Adams Media,
an F+W Publications Company
57 Littlefield Street, Avon, MA 02322.
U.S.A.
www.adamsmedia.com

ISBN 10: 1-60550-031-3
ISBN 13: 978-1-60550-031-7

Printed in the United States of America.

J I H G F E D C

Library of Congress Cataloging-in-Publication Data is available from the publisher.

This publication is designed to provide accurate and authoritative information with regard to the subject matter covered. It is sold with the understanding that the publisher is not engaged in rendering legal, accounting, or other professional advice. If legal advice or other expert assistance is required, the services of a competent professional person should be sought.
—From a *Declaration of Principles* jointly adopted by a Committee of the American Bar Association and a Committee of Publishers and Associations

Many of the designations used by manufacturers and sellers to distinguish their product are claimed as trademarks. Where those designations appear in this book and Adams Media was aware of a trademark claim, the designations have been printed with initial capital letters.

Certain sections of this book deal with activities and devices that would be in violation of various federal, state, and local laws if actually carried out or constructed. We do not advocate the breaking of any law. This information is for entertainment purposes only. We recommend that you contact your local law enforcement officials before undertaking any project based upon any information obtained from this book. We are not responsible for, nor do we assume any liability for, damages resulting from the use of any information in this book.

Interior photographs:
Conceptual Cues © brand x pictures
Whimsical Pop Ins © Comstock
Home & Family © Corbis
Business Office © stockbyte

This book is available at quantity discounts for bulk purchases.
For information, please call
1-800-289-0963.

This book is dedicated to our wives, our mothers,
and to God for blessing us with such incredible talent.

contents

introduction

what the f*#!
is wtf?

-vi-

chapter one

the everydays
of life

-I-

chapter two

out on
the town

-31-

chapter three

workin' for
the man

-67-

chapter four

dealing with
money trouble

-87-

chapter five

traveling at
home and abroad

-103-

chapter six

keeping it
in the family

-127-

chapter seven

in the
bedroom

-147-

chapter eight

dealing with
the mrs.

-171-

chapter nine

there goes the
neighborhood

-187-

chapter ten

tech
troubles

-209-

thanks and
apologies

-233-

Introduction

What the F*#! Is WTF?

W TF? Even if you've never actually said it, you probably know what it stands for. But if you are one of the few people who isn't familiar with the acronym, you might be saying to yourself, "What the f*#!?"—we rest our case. WTF has deep roots. Few people know that legendary Roman ruler Julius Caesar coined the term. Turning toward Brutus moments before his death, he said unto his former friend, "Et tu, Brutus. WTF?" Unfortunately, these profound words were lost to history until archeologists uncovered the ancient city of Pompeii. There, beneath the rubble left from the violent eruption of Mount Vesuvius, three letters stood frozen in time, perfectly preserved

on a once vibrantly colorful fresco: *WTF?*—Julius Caesar.

Indeed, the phrase has quite a history. Today, while we don't have Attila the Hun ravaging the world, you'll still encounter plenty of situations that make you want to scream, "WTF!" From being out of condoms when you finally need one to being harassed by telemarketers, we've compiled 101 of the most aggravating and infuriating situations contemporary life has to offer as well as the tools you need to survive them. Situations that make you say—you guessed it—WTF?

the everydays
of life

1. You Can't Remember Where You Parked

You've been through this several thousand times before, but you can't seem to learn your lesson. So there you are—again—in the middle of a crowded parking lot without the vaguest idea where you parked. Forgetting you parked in the Orange lot, section G2, Row A is one thing, but not even remembering what floor you're on is incredibly stupid.

Nevertheless, here's what to do:

The WTF Approach to Finding Your F*#!-ing Car

➤ OPTION #1: *Think Carefully*

If you were a 2006 Nissan Maxima, where would you be?

➤ OPTION #2: *Report It Stolen*

Go get a drink and let the cops find it. If they don't, you'll be able to collect the insurance money and get a new one that doesn't have french fries stuck between the seats.

➤ OPTION #3: *Wait Until the Place Closes*

With fewer cars on the lot, you should be able to find yours. This won't work if you misplaced your car at O'Hare.

➤ OPTION #4: *Find Someone to Drive You Around*

The security guy will probably do it, or you could call a cab . . . but

you might want to take this opportunity to pick up sympathetic women instead.

➤ OPTION #5: *Make a Spectacle*

Walk around like a jackass with your arm in the air hitting the unlock button on your key and looking for your car's lights to flash. If you don't have one of those electronic keys, your car should be ugly enough to spot.

➤ OPTION #6: *Borrow Another Car*

If there's no security guard and you can't find anyone to drive you around, hotwire another car and borrow it until you find yours.

➤ OPTION #7: *Check your Blackberry*

See if you made a note about where you parked. What good is it to have ridiculously expensive, portable electronic instruments if you don't use them to solve the most ordinary of issues? Maybe you should get one for your kid and make it his job to keep track of your life.

➤ OPTION #8: *Buy the Place*

Close it for renovation. The sole remaining car should be yours.

IN THE FUTURE . . .

Use mnemonic devices. Try to memorize the location of your car based on words you make from the letter and number. If you park in H3, think of three horses. If you park in M16, think of the gun. If you park in F69 . . .

2. Your Dry Cleaner Ruins Your Clothing and Won't Pay for It

If you've ever had a suit or a shirt shrunk down to a miniature version of what it was by an incompetent dry cleaner, you've undoubtedly heard the same bullshit explanation the employee gives everyone. "It was like that already." Sound familiar? Well, now imagine the line is spoken in a thick accent and it will hit home.

The WTF Approach to Getting Some F*#!-ing Money for Your Ruined Clothes

Dry cleaners are some of the biggest liars on the planet and we at WTF have vowed to put an end to their criminal acts. Here's what to do the next time your shirt ends up fit for a Ken doll.

> **STEP #1: Get Them to Admit Fault**

Naturally, they're going to deny it the first few times you complain, expecting you to walk away and shrug your shoulders. Don't. Keep complaining. To prove your case,

take off the shirt you're wearing and hold it next to the shrunken one. Rhetorically ask, "Did I gain fifty pounds and grow five inches in a week?"

> **STEP #2: *Protest***

Make a spectacle of yourself and hold up the line. Show the other customers what the cleaner has done. In front of a jury of your peers, with the evidence of the crime, the dry cleaner may give in and offer you credit for more dry cleaning. If you settle for the credit, don't send them anything they haven't cleaned before.

> **STEP #3: *Sue Them***

A dry cleaner will almost never reimburse you for your loss outside of court. If they did, they'd go out of business. So unless it's worth the hassle, you'll have to forget about it.

IN THE FUTURE . . .

Don't go to discount cleaners. Take your Armani suit to the best dry cleaner in town. If you thought you could just pay $4.50 to get it cleaned properly, think again.

3. You Find a Booger in Your Breakfast Sandwich

Everyone knows that eating at fast food joints is about the worst thing you can do for your body outside of hardcore drugs. And just like when you're about to push a spoonful of H into your veins, when you're about to chow down on some fast food, you don't want to spot a booger in it—even though the booger is probably better for you. Other than the oink, that sausage patty contains whey protein concentrate, water, salt, corn syrup solids, sugar, spices, dextrose, spice extractives, caramel color, BHA and BHT, propyl gallate and citric acid, and monosodium glutamate—which even the Chinese place on the corner stopped using . . . or so they say.

The WTF Approach to Eating F*#!-ing Fast Food

Here's the simplest solution: If you find something suspicious in your sandwich, throw it out and go to a goddamn deli. It's your fault for going there in the first place. *Never return your fast food.*

Fast food restaurants employ the barely employable, and the more you complain, the more bodily fluids they'll try to sneak into your belly.

> **OPTION #1:** *Eat Food That You Can See Them Make*

You can get a good look at the assembly line at Subway, most Taco Bells, and some burger joints. If you can watch the whole process, you can be pretty sure that it's safe—unless they jerk off in the mayonnaise after hours.

> **OPTION #2:** *Don't Eat Fast Food*

It doesn't taste that good, it's bad for you, and it makes you fat. If you're in a rush and can't sit down for a good meal, grab an apple or just skip lunch.

Fast-Food Pyramid

Employee's body fluids and hair group:
Use sparingly

Condiment group:
2–3 servings per day

Processed cheese group:
2–4 servings per day

Miscellaneous animal body parts group:
3–5 servings per day

Lard group:
6–11 servings per day

4. A Panhandler Won't Leave You Alone

"**B**rother, can you spare a dime?" It'd be nice if panhandlers were that polite. They might even get a buck or two as a result. But they're not. Usually it's more like this:

HIM: "Got a quarter?"
YOU: "No."
HIM: "Come on. I'm hungry."
YOU: "Sorry."
HIM: "I'm a Vietnam vet."
YOU: "I still don't have any money for you."

HIM: "I have cancer."
YOU: "Yep. Still nothing in my pockets."
HIM: "And AIDS."
YOU: "Still nothing, bro."
HIM: "No? Then f*#! you!"

Still, it's not easy to say no, but you can't give to all of them. If you did, you'd be out of cash in a minute—half a minute in San Francisco, where the homeless population is only rivaled by the homosexual population.

> **NOTE:** Sometimes you'll see people who are both homeless *and* homosexual. You can always tell them apart: They're the ones with the nicest cardboard boxes and the most organized shopping carts filled with crap.

The WTF Approach to Dealing with F*#!-ing Panhandlers

➤ **STEP #1: *Don't Look***

If you do your best to avoid eye contact, then not giving is easier.

➤ **STEP #2: *Lie and Say, "I'm sorry, man."***

Apologize and pretend to look in your pockets as if you would have given him something but you just can't today.

➤ **STEP #3: *Give Him a Lecture on "Personal Responsibility"***

If you have some free time, take out Ralph Waldo Emerson's essay on "Self-Reliance" and read to him. The delicate prose and stirring sentiment will no doubt inspire him—to kill you, probably!

➤ **STEP #4: *Give Some Money— to the Deserving Ones***

If you're like us, every couple of years you wake up and feel generous. But since you can't give to everyone, you have to be choosy. Here's our hierarchy for handing out to the homeless:

THE LEGLESS OR ARMLESS

Give to amputees first, since their lives are the most depressing.

THE REAL VETERANS

There are too many homeless veterans in this country, but how can you tell which ones are lying about serving and which ones are the genuine, f*#!-ed-up article? Ask them. Find out what branch of the armed services he supposedly served in and what company, battalion, etc. If you still suspect him of lying, ask for further proof like dog tags or an old picture of him with a really lame buzz cut.

BLACK OVER WHITE

Given the historical persecution of blacks and minorities, you should give to a black homeless person over a white homeless person, all things being equal. Think of it as affirmative action for losers.

THE TALENTED ONES

Can your homeless person do tricks? If he can dance or do a magic trick, he should be rewarded with a buck or two.

Always Give if You're on a Date

If you are on a date with a girl, always give a panhandler something unless he's really rude or obnoxious. You can never look too nice in front of someone that you want to impress. A buck or so is a small price to pay to get laid. Now, her $14 chocolate martinis, on the other hand . . .

A Bum Story

Match the panhandler's story with the real story.

A. Says he's a Vietnam vet with diabetes.

B. Says he's a former college professor with cancer.

C. Says he's a schizophrenic with no legs.

1. He's really a dumb drunk with cirrhosis.

2. He's a schizophrenic crack-head with no legs.

3. He's really a junkie with diabetes.

Answers: A: 3, B: 1, C: 2

> ### WHAT THE F*#! IS UP WITH . . .
> #### ASIAN PANHANDLERS
>
> Why is it that you never see an Asian panhandler in America? Go to Asia and all they do is ask you for shit, but here Asians don't beg for money—apparently they're too busy making it.

5. You're at a Red Light . . . at Night . . . for Five Minutes

You're stopped at a light on an empty street. You've already waited three minutes for this thing to change, but it won't. If you go, you risk a ticket, but the thing isn't changing. It might change in a minute. So you wait.

But it doesn't. Now it's been four minutes and you've decided to go, but you see a car in the distance heading your way. It could be a cop. So you wait.

It wasn't. But now you've been there five minutes. Will it ever change? You decide to go for it. You take your foot off the break, hit the gas, and you make it . . . or do you?

The WTF Approach to F*#!-ing Red Lights

➤ **STEP #1:** *Look Carefully for Cops*

Look in places that you'd hide if you were looking for suckers who'd try to run through a broken light, like behind a bush, in an alley, or in front of a doughnut shop.

➤ **STEP #2:** *Look for Cameras*

You can usually see them. If you see one, don't go. Wait forever if you have to. Don't worry. The city will get right on the broken light . . . in a week or two.

➤ **STEP #3:** *Book Through It*

Put the car in gear, close your eyes, and hit the gas. Open your eyes before you get too far though, bozo.

➤ **STEP #4:** *Complain*

Call the city employees who deal with traffic lights. If you don't know the number, call 911 and they'll direct you. You can also ask their permission to go through the light. Just say that it's an emergency.

6. You Don't Have Any Change for the Meter

We know cities have to make money, but aren't tolls and subway rides and hundreds of different kinds of taxes enough? Do you *really* have to give me a $40 ticket because I didn't have change for my meter? How about making me pay a buck—four times as much as the quarter I didn't have? That would be fair. But $40? The only other times you get this screwed, this fast are when you're late on your credit card payment or need legal advice.

You can beg and cry, but meter maids are as notoriously black-hearted as robber barons, the grim reaper, and teenage boys combined. The best way to fight back is to get a handicapped-parking permit. These little placards will allow you to ignore all but the most serious parking laws—and all you need to do is get an M.D. to vouch for you, limp into your local DMV, and you're set.

Not only can this save you hundreds of dollars a year in parking tickets, you get to park in those conveniently located spaces reserved for, well, you!

Today about 10 percent of drivers in California have handicapped-parking permits. Either there's been a rash of landmine accidents and *Misery*-type assaults or people are wising up.

The WTF Approach to Beating the F*#!-ing Meter System

➤ STEP #1: ~~Kill the Meter Maid!~~

Unfortunately, we cannot endorse or condone, under any circumstances or for any reason, any act of violence—such as the beating, stabbing, stoning, drawing and quartering, running over, shooting, tazering, pepper spraying, drowning, throwing darts at, covering him with gasoline and lighting him on fire, or sticking his face in a George Foreman Grill—on parking-enforcement agents. Just give them a taste of their own medicine instead. Follow the prick home and move *his* car across the street on street-sweeping day.

HOW TO SPOT A METER MAID AS A KID ...

- Starts fires
- Wets the bed
- Is cruel to animals

Or is that list for serial killers?

➤ STEP #2: *Kill the Meter*

Since the first step isn't legal—yet—the next best thing is to take the power away from the machine. Rise up! Don't let some coin-eating piece of metal tell you when you have to leave happy hour. All you need is a business card, some muscle, and a set of *cajones*.

First, fold your business card in half, and then fold it in half again, and then one more time, and then press it down as hard as you can. Now slide your meter-killer into the coin slot as you turn the crank and feed the monster your rigid cardboard square—this is where the muscle comes into play. If you succeed, the crank should twist and an "Out of Order" flag will fly up. *Victory!*

WTFACT: There are approximately 100,000 parking meters in Los Angeles. That's about one for every victim of police brutality.

7. Telemarketers Won't Stop Harassing You

Telemarketers are horrible people. There is no reason to treat them like human beings, let alone nicely. So say whatever you want to them.

The WTF Approach to Handling F*#!-ing Telemarketers

If you want them to stop calling, find out what company the telemarketer is with, the name of the caller, and say, "Never call me again. Take my name out of your database. If you do not, I will sue and file harassment charges against you and the company you work for." Or if you want to have a little fun with them, try one of these:

➤ OPTION ONE: *Propose*

Ask the telemarketer if she'll marry you. If she says "no," ask her if she's gay.

➤ OPTION TWO: *Tell Her You're Interested*

But keep putting her on hold.

➤ OPTION THREE: *Try to Sell Her Something*

Tell her that you have an interesting business proposition for her. Explain that for an investment of just $100,000, she could get in to the lucrative and exciting world of door-to-door dinosaur egg sales.

> **OPTION FOUR:** *Graphically Explain that You're Busy*

Tell the telemarketer that you're "balls deep in some sweet ass" and to call back when you "ain't f*#!-in'."

> **OPTION FIVE:** *Sing "Moon River" to Her*

Everyone likes Henry Mancini and Johnny Mercer. Right?

> **OPTION SIX:** *Tell Her that Nature Calls*

Tell her that you "gotta shit" and to call back in six hours when you're done.

> **OPTION SEVEN:** *Tell "Yo Momma" Jokes*

Start with this favorite: "Yo' momma's so fat that yo' pops has to roll her in flour to find her wet spot."

> **OPTION EIGHT:** *Ask for a Discount*

Ask her if she has any special deals just for necrophiliacs.

> **OPTION NINE:** *Confuse Her*

Tell her that, yes, you are the person she's looking for, but that you no longer live here anymore.

> **OPTION TEN:** *Scare the Shit Out of Her*

Introduce yourself as Sheriff McNeil, and tell her that she's just called the scene of a kidnapping. Immediately begin interrogating her as to how she knows the missing person (you). Ask her if she's the kidnapper and to go over her demands. When she starts freaking out and says she's just a telemarketer, tell her that the call has been traced and that the local authorities will be there shortly.

8. You've Been Dieting for Months and Still Haven't Lost Weight

So you've tried eating all meat, no meat, all carbs, no carbs, diet pills, just soup and, maybe once or twice, cocaine—but nothing's helped. Know why? Because diets are bullshit, that's why. Want to drop some pounds? Stop eating like a fat pig and exercise. Simple.

The WTF Approach to Losing Some F*#!-ing Weight

➤ **STEP #1:** *Quit Making Excuses*

Stop with the thyroid problem nonsense or saying that you have really "bad metabolism." You can always lose weight, so just do it!

➤ **STEP #2:** *Never Shop When You're Hungry*

This is the worst thing you can do. Before long your cart will be filled not with healthy vegetables and low-fat food, but with six bags of Cheetos, cookies, doughnuts, and, just because you haven't tried them yet, some disgusting new flavor of potato chips.

➤ **STEP #3:** *Get Some Therapy*

Who knows, you could be eating like a pig because your daddy was mean to you or your mommy didn't give you enough attention. Find out what the hell is wrong with you so you don't have to drown your sorrows in a chocolate milkshake and a banana split.

➤ STEP #4: *Get Another Addiction*

You can take up drinking or smoking or drugs to replace your food addiction. Of course, you might end up dead from an overdose as a fat, pill-popping, cigarette-smoking drunk. Think Elvis.

➤ STEP #5: *Staple Your Stomach*

If you have the dough and you're too lazy to hit the gym, getting your stomach stapled is a fine way to lose weight. Sure it's dangerous, but so is riding a bicycle.

WHAT THE F*#! IS UP WITH . . .
FAT AMERICA

This country is by far the fattest in the world. Just look around. This epidemic is a reflection of our gluttonous lifestyle and lack of self-discipline. It's also a reflection of how hard we work. Most employees don't even get a lunch break to eat something leisurely, so they're forced to shove down a sandwich at their desk like an animal trapped in a cage. So file a class action against the man for clogging your arteries, giving you four chins, and making it physically impossible for you to put on your socks. That's the real fat American way.

New Diets . . .

As we said, diets don't work, but they help get you started. Here are a few new ones to jumpstart your weight loss.

Bug Diet: Fat bugs. If your house is infested with termites, eat them first. Then check out "Your New House Is Infested with Termites" on page 196.

Water Diet: Whenever you're hungry, drink water. Even if you can't keep it up, at least you'll be a fat pig with clear skin.

Hair Diet: Eat your hair. Most cats are sleek and thin for a reason.

Pussy Diet: F*#! it—just eat a cat instead.

9. Your Date Stands You Up

We know what you're thinking: *You're ugly and no one likes you.* Right? Well, *she* certainly thought so when she stood you up. Even if that's true, remember that there is always someone more unattractive and unappealing than you are. So there is a special (or not-so-special) person out there for everyone—even you—and she definitely won't stand you up . . . once you find her.

The WTF Approach to Securing a F*#!-ing Date

> **OPTION #1: *Lower Your Standards***

If your standards are too high, you don't deserve to get laid. If you're 5'6", bald, and work at Kinko's, you're not going to be pulling in too many supermodels unless you're hung like a horse. If you are, make a photocopy of it and keep it in your wallet at all times.

> **OPTION #2: *Get Help***

Maybe you could use a little makeover. Call one of those shows like *Queer Eye for the Straight Guy* that specialize in making

unattractive people look good. Or better yet, just become queer yourself. Gay guys can always get laid no matter how vile they are.

➤ OPTION #3: *Make a Good-Looking Friend*

Go out on the town with a cool guy that gets chicks so, by proxy, maybe you can, too. Feed off the scraps like the dog that you are.

➤ OPTION #4: *Join* **Match.com**

Maybe you met your first date on the site—but she stood you up. News flash: You probably weren't using the site right. Make sure to put your income level at $150,000 plus and never, ever say you're shorter than 5'10".

For you girls, just try not to look too smart—brains are icky to most guys. Think about it, would *you* fuck a brain?

➤ OPTION #5: *Try Speed Dating*

With this idea, you may get turned down by multiple women in five minutes, but they're at least showing up. Dating is a numbers game anyway, so speed dating is to your benefit. If you meet a million girls, one of them will let you in between her legs.

Remember, though: First impressions are lasting impressions. And, when you only have a couple of minutes, you've got to get their attention quickly.

So say this:

"Hi, I'm [fill in name here]. I'm rich, well educated, and hung like a horse."

If you *are* hung like a horse, whip it out. Make sure to smile—women love a guy with a great smile.

➤ OPTION #6: *Date a Blind Chick*

Not only can she not see you, the idea is kind of hot.

➤ OPTION #7: *Join Sex Addicts Anonymous*

You might feel out of your league, but these floozies won't stand anyone up.

for the ladies . . .

For you gals, getting a date isn't as difficult—but getting stood up is just as painful. Maybe you're getting too old? In which case, you should be knitting a sweater and playing with one of your ten cats instead of being out on the prowl.

➤ OPTION #8: *Go to Thailand*

Just go, pussy will find *you*.

➤ OPTION #9: *Give Up*

Maybe you were stood up for a reason. Join a monastery and become celibate. If you can't get laid, you might as well fool around with God and gardening.

10. You Finish Your Cigarette and There's No Ashtray in Sight

Life is tough enough for smokers. They die earlier, they spend extra cash on their habit, and they smell like shit. So why make it harder for them by implementing fines when they toss their cigarette on the sidewalk or out of a car on the highway? There's no excuse for such nonsense. That's why if you are a smoker and you can't find an ashtray, we at WTF give you permission to toss your cigarette butt on the ground wherever you are—your in-laws' house included.

But for those of you who are environmentally conscious, here are some other options:

The WTF Approach to Ashing Out Your F*#!-ing Butt

➤ OPTION #1: *Put It Out on Your Hand*

Come on, tough guy, show your stuff and impress your lady friend by putting out a lit cigarette on the palm of your hand. The trick is to keep the cigarette in motion the whole time. Try it at home first—please!

➤ OPTION #2: *Use Your Tongue*

If you are *really* cool, put it out on your tongue. Even cooler? Put it out in your f*#!-ing eye.

➤ OPTION #3: *Eat It*

Tobacco is natural—it was put here by God for our consumption. So if you like organic food, chop up the cigarette and shove it down your throat.

➤ OPTION #4: *F*#! It*

Yeah, we know this is weird and hard to do, but try anyway. It will definitely be hot.

Cement Isn't That *Flammable*

News flash for morons: There is no need to step on a burning cigarette butt on the sidewalk. You are not saving anyone's life; you are just pissing people off. Sidewalks are made out of cement, jackass, not papier mâché. Get a grip and get a life. You're not a vigilante; you're just an obnoxious asshole.

And another thing: Nothing ruins an ecosystem more than cementing it over. So what f*#!-ing difference does it make if you toss a butt on the ground? Come on!

WHAT SIDE ARE YOU ON?

FAMOUS SMOKERS

Winston Churchill

Albert Einstein

Gunter Grass

John F. Kennedy

George Orwell

Franklin Delano Roosevelt

Jean Paul Sartre

Vincent Van Gogh

Oscar Wilde

FAMOUS NONSMOKERS

Adolf Hitler

Think about that the next time you light or *don't* light up.

11. The Salt Cap Wasn't Screwed On and You Dump It on Your Meal

Salt is essential for human survival. It's a preservative and a flavor enhancer. It's in almost everything that's good: chips, soda, ham, milk, and, of course, in true WTF fashion: cum. Roman soldiers used to be paid in salt (sometimes, cum). But that doesn't mean you want a cup of it on your dinner (neither salt nor cum). When someone forgets, even if it's you, to screw the top of a saltshaker on properly, it can ruin a meal. That is, unless you're armed with a thorough knowledge of WTF.

The WTF Approach to F*#!-ing Salt-Covered Food

➤ OPTION #1: *Return It*

If you're at a restaurant, they'll probably make you a new order, even though it's not really their fault. Just ask nicely. If they refuse, you could always try to pay in salt (and you can certainly tip in salt).

➤ OPTION #2: *Give It Away*

Give it to the homeless guy who's always begging on your block. That'll shut him up.

➤ OPTION #3: *Serve It to the Fam'*

If it happens while you're cooking and are tired of always making dinner, serve it up anyway with a nice parsley garnish and glass of fine merlot. If they ask why it's so salty, ask, "It's salty?" You'll be off the hook forever.

➤ OPTION #4: *Take It to the Track*

Go to the racetrack and give it to nine horses. Bet on the tenth.

IN THE FUTURE . . .

Be careful. Hindsight is 20/20—next time you reach for the saltshaker, check the f*#!-ing top.

➤ OPTION #5: *Give the Gift of Salt*

If you have horrible neighbors, leave it on their doorstep as a gift.

➤ OPTION #6: *Teach a Lesson*

If your wife is neglecting your needs, serve it to her while telling the story of Abraham's wife Sarah, who was turned into a pillar of salt by God as punishment for her disobedience.

➤ OPTION #7: *Try Your Luck*

If you're down on your luck, throw the dish over your left shoulder. That should be good for 1,000 years of good luck.

Finally, if you find your food covered in salt, be sure to take it with a grain of salt.

12. You Can't Pull Down Your Pants to Crap Because Someone Peed on the Floor

That burrito you had for lunch is talking to you. And it's getting louder by the minute. Finally, you find a restroom, just to see that some animal pissed all over the floor, making it a hazard to pull down your pants. If you can hold it until you find a clean bathroom, feel free. If you can't, try this.

The WTF Approach to Shitting in a F*#!-ing Piss-Ridden Stall

➤ STEP #1: *Roll 'em Up*

If you're wearing jeans, you might be able to keep them off the floor. Slacks are a different story, as they are flimsier and harder to keep in place. You can try rolling them up, but they might not stay that way.

➤ STEP #2: *Soak It Up*

Use the paper towels (if there are none, use toilet seat covers) on the floor to soak up the urine and protect your pants. You could also use toilet paper, if there's enough. Keep in mind that toilet paper is much thinner, and you'll need more of it.

➤ STEP #3: *Hang 'em Up*

If there are neither paper towels nor toilet seat covers, but there's a dispenser for either of those things, take off your pants and hang them on the empty dispenser. If there is no such dispenser, you can place your pants on the sink, but proceed with caution. The sinks in public restrooms are often as filthy as the toilets.

➤ STEP #4: *Tie 'em Up*

If you can't find a clean place to put your pants, you can tie the legs around your neck. Be sure to empty your pockets beforehand. If you're into asphyxiophilia, kill two birds with one stone—tie them tight and jerk off while you're at it.

➤ STEP #5: *Shit in the Sink*

If you're worried about wrinkling your pants and the sink is too dirty to place your pants on, then shit in the sink. It's filthy anyway. Also, legs dangling, your pants are protected from the bathroom floor. Make sure there is adequate space between your asshole and the sink. You don't want to shit all over yourself. If you do, turn the faucet on lukewarm and enjoy a makeshift bidet. Once you shit this way, *mon ami*, you'll never use the toilet again.

13. Your Favorite TV Show Is Cancelled

It's often sad when a show ends, but when a show is cancelled prematurely it can be traumatic. You'll never learn what happens to your favorite characters and you'll have nothing to do on Thursday nights. But just because television executives pulled the plug doesn't mean you have to wallow in your loss forever. You can either learn to let go or learn to fight back.

The WTF Approach to Handling the Cancellation of Your Favorite F*#!-ing Show

➤ OPTION #1: *Get Active*

Start a letter-writing campaign to get your show back. Create a website that encourages other fans to write to the studio and everyone involved in the production.

➤ OPTION #1.5: *Get Really Active*

Take it further by banding together with other diehards and picketing outside the studio. If successful, consider using these organizing skills for a cause that's not insanely stupid.

➤ OPTION #2: *Get a New Favorite Show*

Whatever your favorite show was, there's probably a comparable show you haven't yet seen, whether it's new or old. If you liked *Star Trek*, watch one of the half-dozen reincarnations of the franchise or *Battle Star Galactica*. If you liked *The Office*, watch the other *The Office*. If you liked *Beverly Hills 90210*, you're a moron.

➤ OPTION #3: *Watch Old Episodes Over and Over*

If the series is long enough, you can probably watch it several times before you get tired of it—wasting weeks of your life.

➤ OPTION #4: *Write Fan Fiction*

If you are truly sick, reading and writing fan fiction is another option. You can even write yourself in. You can help your heroes keep New York City's streets safe by locking up murderers, travel the universe in an intergalactic space ship, and help save lives by solving very complex and mysterious medical cases. Plus, you can have yourself sleep with the main character just like you've imagined so many times before.

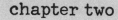

out on the town

14. Some Loudmouth at the Movies Won't Shut Up

Everyone loves the movies. There's nothing like the smell of the popcorn, the cool chill of the theatre, and the possibility—however remote—that your date will give you some action if you nudge her enough. But there's one thing that always looms over a potentially wonderful movie: the chance that some schmuck will spoil the escapist experience and waste your ten bucks by opening his stupid fat mouth and blabbering. And all you can think is: Seriously, WTF?

Doesn't he know the three laws of movie etiquette?

THREE LAWS OF MOVIE ETIQUETTE

1. Shut the f*#! up and watch the film, schmuck.

2. Shut the f*#! up and watch the film, schmuck.

3. Shut the f*#! up and watch the film, schmuck.

The WTF Approach to Shutting Him the F*#! Up

For those of you who aren't schmucks, here's a step-by-step method for dealing with one:

> **STEP #1:** *The* **Shh!**

Shh! the schmuck without looking at him—no reason to reveal your identity at first.

> **STEP #2:** *The Turn and* **Shh!**

Shh! again, but this time turn to the schmuck, thus revealing your identity. This tells the schmuck that he does not live in a vacuum. The average movie schmuck will stop after this second step, as the "turn and *shh!*" produces a certain embarrassment and shame—even for schmucks.

> **STEP #3:** *The Polite Request*

Turn and look the schmuck square in the eye. Pause for a second and stare so he knows you mean business. Then, in a polite yet noticeably restrained tone, ask the schmuck to, "Please be quiet."

> **STEP #4:** *The Command*

If step three doesn't work, then it's official: You are dealing with a real f*#!-ing schmuck here. This means you've got to step it up in order to save your movie experience, not to mention the experience of your fellow non-schmucks trying to watch the film, too. Don't let them or yourself down. Stand up and say exactly what you meant all along: "Shut the f*#! up and watch the picture, schmuck!"

NOTE: While *schmuck* is used here for the purposes of consistency, you may substitute whichever insult you choose. However, we don't condone the use of any derogatory slurs regarding race, ethnicity, gender, or sexual orientation in Step #4 . . . that's Step #5.

Factors to Consider Before Telling the Schmuck Off

Let's face it. Some people are just too scary for us to tell off. Sometimes we've got to bite our tongue not out of courtesy, but out of self-preservation. Here are a few things to check before you push the prick too far:

- Height, weight, and muscle density of the schmuck

- Number of schmucks with the schmuck

- Location of the theatre—safe or not-so-safe neighborhood

- Clothing of the schmuck—look out for blue or red outfits that may suggest gang affiliation

15. Finally, a Hot Girl Hits On You . . . but She's a Hooker

A real hottie comes up to you at a bar and starts chatting you up. She's laughing at your jokes, touching you when she talks, looking at you deeply. You ask if she wants to go back to your place, when she spills the beans—the hooker beans. Sure, you could always say "No, thank you," but this isn't a guide on how to be a good little boy or girl.

Most hookers you'll see on the streets probably aren't for you. They're toothless or legless or have a fat schlong under their skirt. But every once in a while, a really hot-looking hooker will want to do you for a couple hundred bucks. This is when WTF comes in, oh, so handy.

The WTF Approach to Scoring with a F*#!-ing Hooker

➤ **STEP #1: *Stay Local***

If your date wants to drive out to the middle of the Mojave Desert, you better pass. Sure, maybe she'll blow you on the way there and during your drive back to town. But then again, she could also just as easily take your wallet and car and leave you stranded bare-ass in the middle of nowhere.

➤ STEP #2: *Get a Room*

The last thing you need is to go to jail on a laundry list of baloney laws. If you're going to splurge, you might as well pay for a room at the Motel 6, too.

➤ STEP #3: *Question Her*

Before you talk about money, ask her if she's a cop. If she says "no," ask her to grab your junk. This shows both of you that the other isn't a policeman. If she does that, you can be pretty sure she's not there to protect and serve—just to serve.

***WTF*FACT:** In Sweden, selling sex isn't a crime, but buying it is a crime. The Swedes view hookers as exploited victims. Suckers. • In the United States, prostitution is legal in parts of Nevada and in parts of Rhode Island. • In Hungary, prostitutes are union-ized. This gives a whole new meaning to "Union Job." • In the Sudan, you can get the death penalty for prostitution. Then again, when you live in Darfur, you can get the death penalty for pretty much anything

➤ STEP #4: *Remember—No Glove, No Love*

If you're going to get nasty with a girl that does it for money, you better rock a rubber. There are more than twenty-five STDs float-ing around these days, and none of them gives you super powers.

WHAT THE F*#! IS UP WITH . . .
GLAMORIZED PROSTITUTION

After *Pretty Woman* glamorized prostitu-tion, too many young girls started believ-ing that if they could just go to Hollywood and become a whore, everything would turn up roses. But that ain't the truth. The chances of a street hooker riding off into the sunset in a white limousine with Richard Gere are slim. There's a better chance she'll wind up hacked into pieces and tossed in the back of a pickup truck.

16. A Really Drunk Girl Hits On You

Yes, it was *her* choice to drink. Yes, she did hit on *you*. And yes, who's to say whether or not she would have hit on you if she was sober.

You can find a way to rationalize anything. That's what human beings do, and why we are capable of such terrible things. But even though it was her choice to drink and even though you aren't doing anything illegal, taking advantage of a drunk girl who's about to pass out and vomit all over the place is probably wrong. Yes, it's hard to say no to sex—and even harder when you are feeling tipsy, too.

The WTF Approach to F*#!-ing Figuring Out if She's Too Drunk to F*#!

➤ **STEP #1:** *Determine Her Level of Sobriety*

While you don't have to go so far as carrying a breathalyzer in your pocket (though that's actually a really good idea), there are other ways to determine the girl's level of drunkenness. Walking the line, standing on one leg, and following a flashlight with your eyes have

all long been used by the police to determine the level of alcohol consumption, so try one of those tests. If she passes them, thumbs up. If she doesn't pass, get her a cup of coffee, and try again in a half hour.

➤ STEP #2: *Drink More*

So she's passed your field sobriety test, but she's still way more wasted than you. While the question of taking advantage of a *really* drunk girl is answered—you're not, she's passed the tests—you are still way too sober for any entertaining sex. (Sober sex with a drunk girl is like poking a dead jellyfish—where's the excitement?)

If you match her to the point where you are equally drunk, it'll make things a lot more interesting. So, drink up.

➤ STEP #3: *FUI*

Now that you're both well lubricated, it's time for some f*#!-ing under the influence. Take your cue from middle school multiplication, a drunk f*#!-ing a drunk equals a positive experience.

And just like middle school multiplication, you won't remember it.

17. All Geared Up to Party, but You Can't Get in Da' Club

Yeah, son. This club is poppin', yo. There's mad fly honeys everywhere. You got your new gear on, mad loot in your pocket, and you brought your best game. If only you could get in the doors. Instead you're stuck outside, and it doesn't look like they lettin' you in. What to do, foo'?

The WTF Approach to Getting in Da' F*#!-ing Club

➤ OPTION #1: *Find Women*

Find a group of eight scantily clad, hot women to walk in with. But then again, if you can get eight hot chicks at will, you'd already be on the list.

➤ OPTION #2: *Slip the Bouncer Some Cash*

If you want to know how much to give the bouncer, use this formula:

> (Number of men in line x 2) + (number of women in line ÷ 3) + (cover charge x 1.5)
> = the necessary amount of loot

If you can't do this in your head, you should probably stay home and brush up on your algebra.

➤ OPTION #3: *Go Back to the Pub*

It's almost as good as being surrounded by beautiful women at the hottest club in town. Strike up a good chat with Mickey the barkeep. If you're lucky, he'll tell you the story about the time when he caught the marlin mounted on the wall, or how he lost his right hand in 'Nam. Make sure to play Billy Joel's "Piano Man" on the jukebox and think about all your shattered dreams. End the night dancing with a fat college chick to "Livin' on a Prayer," which, apparently, you are.

WHAT THE F*#! IS UP WITH . . .
BOUNCERS

Hey, bouncers! Just because you decide who is cool enough to get in doesn't mean you're cool. You're doormen, not celebrities. Get over yourselves. You make twelve bucks an hour, for crying out loud . . . plus the tips people like us have to dish out.

➤ OPTION #4: *Leave Your Neighborhood*

You might not be cool enough for the East Village, but you'll probably fit in nicely in Jersey. Or better yet, relocate someplace where they think that even Jersey is cool.

➤ OPTION #5: *Ditch Your Friend*

It might not be you. It could be your friend. Sure, he's nice, but ever since you started hanging out with him, you've gotten half the chicks you used to and you can't get in anywhere cool. Hang out with him Tuesday afternoons, not Saturday nights. Replace him with someone better for the weekends. But be careful not to find someone too much better or you'll wind up alone on Tuesday afternoons—and Saturday nights.

18. You're Out on a Date and You Run Into an Ex

Boy, you're into this girl. She's cute, fun, and seems like she'll be great in the sack. So, you take her out for a night on the town, dinner at your favorite place, dancing at the coolest bar, and then, with a little luck and a lot of tequila, wild sex all night.

You pick her up from her place, and she's as hot as can be. The conversation is good, and she seems way into you—you start to hope she suggests skipping the dancing altogether. But as you pull in to the Denny's down the street from your place, you see a very familiar Jetta parked in the lot.

Once inside, you see a girl you used to go out with, and before you can suggest another restaurant, you've got a glass of ice water in your face.

The WTF Approach to Not Running into Your F*#!-ing Exes

➤ OPTION #1: Expand Your Playing Field

If you've spent five years bagging the women that live within a two-mile radius of your house, you can't be that surprised if you run into them. Expanding your stomping ground means more new girls and a lot less exes.

WTFACT: Los Angeles has a population density of 8,205 per square mile. If you don't travel outside of a two-mile radius from your house, you have about 100,000 people in your world. Half are women, giving us 50,000. 7.5% are within 5 years of your age, making our number 3,750. Ten percent are gay (3,375). A third are married or have a boyfriend (2,230). Some 15% are overweight (1,900), and half of them are ugly (950). Of those thousand girls, half have serious emotional issues, and of the 475 girls that remain, only a handful that would ever go out with you. Now, expand that to ten miles and you have 2,500,000 people, giving you a total of 11,875 girls in your possible dating pool (twice that if you don't mind psychos). Now isn't that a much sexier number?

➤ OPTION #2: Go Upscale

Chances are, the girls you date don't do fine dining. If you're too lazy to drive across town, pay up and go upscale.

➤ OPTION #3: Make Staying in Cooler

Get a pool table, a fully stocked bar, a 100" plasma television, a chef, a butler, a maid, etc., so that there's no longer any reason to leave your place. If you have problems with exes stopping by, get a Doberman or a shotgun.

This option is also great because, if the level of service you offer at home is better than she can get anywhere else, she'll let you on top of her for as long as you want.

19. You Get Asked Out on a Date and Are Expected to Pay

A first date is a tryout. You don't know each other, and you've gotten together to discover if there's potential. So why should you alone be expected to foot the bill—especially if she was the one who did the asking? If you choose to, good for you. But it isn't fair that she gets to go out for free over and over again. Here's how to avoid paying without ruining your chances to score.

The WTF Approach to F*#!-ing Paying Less

► OPTION #1: *Disappear Before the Check Arrives*

When you see the waiter approaching with the bill, go to the bathroom. Stay in there for a little while. With luck, when you come back, she'll have her card on the table and at least offer to pay half.

► OPTION #2: *Be Up Front*

Let her know that you never pay for first dates. Even if she thinks you're cheap, you have the remainder of the dinner to redeem yourself. This is much better than surprising her at the end. In fact, this setup can alter the natural dynamic and work in your favor. You've established from the very start that it isn't just your job

to impress her; it's also her job to impress you. Who does she think she is, anyway?

➤ OPTION #3: *Cut and Run*

If you don't like her, don't pay for the whole date. Wait until she goes to the bathroom, drop your share on the table, and leave. If she's *really* awful, just leave.

First Dates for Cheapskates

Taco Bell: Everybody likes burritos, and you definitely can foot the bill. But should you, really?

Picnic in the park: Find the cheapest brie in the store, strawberries, and a bottle of André and put it in a backpack. Now you're not cheap, you're romantic.

Rollerskating rink: It'll show that you're young at heart, and if she fits into your ex-girlfriend's roller skates, you'll make out like a bandit.

A hike: It shows you're athletic, and the most you'll be expected to buy is a bottle of water.

The beach: If you live by a beach, you should take her to one. If not, go to the lake. If you don't live by a beach or a lake, you should move.

Three Dates and You're Out

If you are going to be the sole financier of this dating trial period, your investment should start paying dividends by the third date. If she doesn't give it up by then, look elsewhere. It's a global marketplace.

IN THE FUTURE

If you get stuck with the bill, don't go out with her again. Unless "going out" means coming over to play hide the salami.

20. Your Best Friend's Girl Hits On You

She's always flirted with you. She touches your leg when she talks to you. She laughs at all your jokes. When she hugs you, she holds on a little too long. And, most importantly, she just *looks* like she's easy. It was all in fun until the night she whispered in your ear that she wanted you . . . *badly*. What to do, what to do?

Before you act, think of the age-old adage, "bros before hos." But this can be misleading. In some situations, what seems like the wrong thing might be the right thing to do.

The WTF Approach to Handling Your Buddy's F*#!-ing Cock-Hungry Girl

➤ **OPTION #1: *Bang Her and Tell Him***

The first benefit of this is obvious. You get to bang her. The other benefit is less obvious, however. By telling him, you're doing him a world of good. He has a right to know that he's dating an unfaithful and untrustworthy girl. As a true friend, it is your job to get to the bottom of things, to investigate. You've got to make sure that she's

the nasty slut you think she is. It's your obligation to find out and to let him know. After all, what kind of friend would you be if you didn't?

➤ OPTION #2: *Bang Her and Don't Tell Him*

On the other hand, there's no reason to hurt his feelings. It's best to not tell him. He likes the girl and they have a good relationship. So she needs a little dick on the side—big deal. Better you than some random guy she picks up at a club who could have God knows what kind of diseases. Do you really want to put your friend in danger like that? Be a true friend and protect him by having sex with his girl over and over again. Give it to her so hard, so fast, and so often that she won't have the energy to look elsewhere. After all, what kind of friend would you be if you didn't?

➤ OPTION #3: *Don't Bang Her and Tell Him*

What's the matter with you? You can't bang your friend's girl. Do the right thing by keeping your dick in your pants. Now go and tell him like a true friend, so he knows the kind of person he's intimately involved with. After all, what kind of friend would you be if you didn't?

➤ OPTION #4: *Don't Bang Her and Don't Tell Him*

On the other hand . . . it's best not to get involved. It's none of your business and it's not your place to pry into their relationship. Also, he may not believe you, and instead accuse you of trying break up him and his girl. Do the right thing and keep your mouth shut. After all, what kind of friend would you be if you didn't?

NOTE: As you see, you can justify any action you take. So, the real question and determining factor is: Is she *hot,* or not?

21. Your Girlfriend Takes You to the Farmers' Market, Again

WTF is *so* great about a grocery store outside? Shopping for food is a chore, not entertainment. Even clothes shopping, though all straight guys hate it, is better than food shopping. People in this country work more than fifty hours a week and then have to spend the majority of their free time doing stupid chores like grocery shopping. Come the weekend, the one time when maybe, just maybe, you don't have to bust your ass with monotonous shit, you spend it picking out tomatoes on the street sold by a bunch of hicks from out of town? No, thank you. Eating at a nice restaurant and heavy boozing to forget about yet another horrible week of work sounds much more fun.

The WTF Approach to Getting Out of the F*#!-ing Market Trip

➤ **OPTION #1:** *Tell Her You're Sick*

You haven't been feeling well since last Saturday, when as usual, you went to another farmers' market.

➤ **OPTION #2:** *Make the Farmers' Market Too Expensive*

If you buy $500 worth of candy apples, organic corn on a stick, and giant green beans, maybe you can convince her that the farmers' market just isn't in the budget. Instead, suggest one of your favorite upscale steakhouses and an exclusive VIP gentleman's club to save money.

➤ **OPTION #3:** *Starve Yourself for a Day and Go Pig Out*

Fifteen-dollar organic cauliflower never tasted so good.

OTHER THINGS TO DO AT A FARMER'S MARKET . . .

- Make chitchat with hick farmers
- Haggle over the price of an avocado
- Pretend you're having a good time with your girlfriend, chit-chatting with hick farmers and haggling over the price of an avocado.

The Whole Third World Is a Farmer's Market

For all you farmers' market fans, why don't you pack up your shit and head to a Third World country? Locals there shop outside every day (if they're lucky). Know why? Because they don't have f*#!-ing grocery stores.

22. You Just Got a Drink and Some Klutz Knocks It Over

It's exactly where you want to be. It's crowded, it's loud, and the chances of organizing a gangbang look promising. It's your favorite spot and tonight is going great. Then, just when you've forgotten how boring your life is and are actually having fun, some klutz knocks over your drink.

How to react to such a situation depends on your point of view. If you consider your martini glass to be half empty, you might just shrug your shoulders and say, as you usually do, "Oh well, life sucks" and not take action. If you're an upbeat kind of person and see the drink half full, then you've got no other choice then to make the klutz pay up.

The WTF Approach to Dealing with a F*#!-ing Klutz

➤ **STEP #1: *Act Immediately***

Don't waste any time. The klutz might disappear in the crowd. Confront the klutz and tell him what he has done.

➤ **STEP #2: *Make Demands***

Chances are, the klutz will not offer to get you another drink, so demand it right away.

➤ STEP #3: *Knock over the Klutz's Drink*

Sometimes it's best to follow the Old Testament principle of, "an eye for an eye." Knock the klutz's drink all over him. If he gets mad and threatens you, you now have the green light to take Step #4.

WHAT YOUR DRINK SAYS ABOUT HOW YOU'RE GOING TO REACT

Jack Daniel's straight up: If you were really a true Jack lover, you'd probably have hit the klutz *before* he knocked over your drink.

Margarita: Man, you're just there to, like, have a totally good time and, you know, chill out and talk to your buddies and stuff. You don't want to, like, start anything, but that was totally f*#!-ed up, dude.

Martini: You don't really care about the drink. You have money to buy another one. If you do anything, it's to show off.

Pabst Blue Ribbon: You're already broke, so either you get him to buy you a new one or you're going home.

Midori Sour: You couldn't hurt a fly, but you think the klutz's kinda cute . . .

➤ STEP #4: *Aim Low*

If the klutz gets nasty and denies it, threaten him. If this doesn't work, you know you've got to take physical action. *Do not* let the klutz off the hook, no matter what. The best way to win a fight with a klutz is to attack his weakness—balance. Trip the klutz and watch him fall. Then, take the klutz's wallet and buy drinks for you and all your friends.

23. You Get Pulled Over After a Couple Drinks

It could never happen to you, right? Wrong, you fool. Unless you're a teetotaler or you just have a bus pass, you'll eventually get stopped by the cops after a night on the town.

The WTF Approach to Being F*#!-ing Pulled Over

➤ STEP #1: *Swish and Swallow*

Keep mouthwash in your glove box. Some cops won't notice you've had anything to drink if you don't smell like a friggin' sailor.

➤ STEP #2: *Decline the Field Sobriety Test*

If you admit that you're drunk, that's proof in itself. If you deny it, the burden of proof is on them. If they ask you to take a field sobriety test, decline it. The alphabet backward? Alternating bringing each index finger up to the tip of your nose? Putting one foot in front of the other and walking a straight line? Admit it—you'd have trouble doing this without the added performance anxiety.

➤ STEP #3: *The Breathalyzer*

The cop's next move will be to give you a breathalyzer. If you've only had a couple drinks you'll be fine and on your way. However, if you think you might fail, decline.

NOTE: In some jurisdictions the penalty for declining a breathalyzer is a mandatory suspension of your license. But WTF do you think they'll do when they find out you're over the limit? They'll do that and more.

►STEP #4: *The Blood Test*

At this point, the cop will bring you to the station for a blood test. By that time, your blood alcohol level may drop if it was just above the limit.

What Not to Do When You Get Pulled Over

Take cocaine: It makes the alcohol less noticeable— by drawing attention to your powdered nostril and dilated pupils.

Offer a bribe: Your bills can be coke free, or not, depending on how "down" the cop looks.

Hit the gas: You won't get very far, it's a waste of gas, but it does add a dramatic flair.

REMEMBERING RODNEY

" I drink too much. The last time I gave a urine sample it had an olive in it. "

—Rodney Dangerfield

Don't Be MADD, It's Your Fault

Sure, you want to blame the fact that you couldn't find adequate public transportation or the fact that women don't seem to want to have sex with you unless you get them and yourself drunk, but don't be pissed. Since 1980 (the year Mothers Against Drunk Driving was founded), alcohol-related traffic fatalities have decreased by about 44 percent, and MADD has helped save more than 300,000 lives.

WTFACT: About three in every ten Americans will be involved in an alcohol-related crash at some time in their lives. Buckle up.

IN THE FUTURE . . .

Make friends with nerds. Everyone should have at least one friend who is a nerd and doesn't drink—and will drive. Yes, only nerds and ex-alcoholics don't drink.

24. You Meet the Girl of Your Dreams but She's Not Into You

You could always spend more time at the gym, make more money, or develop a personality, but there's an easier way to impress your dream girl: Lie.

Dishonesty is the best policy if you want the hottest women. Plus, chicks lie all the time. They put on makeup, stuff their bras, and say they like a guy with a sense of humor. It's time to get back.

The WTF Approach to Getting the Girl Who's Way Out of Your F*#!-ing League

➤ STEP #1: *Lie About Your Job*

While a novice liar might think he should just pick a job that pays a lot of money, this isn't the best idea. Cater your lie to the venue. If you're at a rock concert and you see a girl you want to impress, be a music producer. If you're at a ball game, be a sports agent. If you're at a Goth club, be a gravedigger. And, if you're at the local Irish bar, be an out-of-work machinist. However, for a lie that will work anywhere, with anyone, being a doctor is best. Everybody respects a doctor.

➤ STEP #2: *Lie About Your Family*

You don't have one. Be the lone stranger who doesn't need anyone to thrive. Be a widower, an orphan, or tell a tragic story about the loss of your first and only child. Your perseverance and show of strength will draw her to you.

➤ STEP #3: *Lie About Your Politics*

Find out what political stance she takes and take the opposite view. If she's pro-choice, be pro-life. If she's for free trade, be a protectionist. If she's against slavery, be for it. This will get her fired up, and hopefully that fire will continue to the bedroom.

Study Your Prey

If you want to take it to the next level, you need to understand exactly who it is you're lying to. Depending on the girl, you'll have to customize your lies to turn you into Mr. Right.

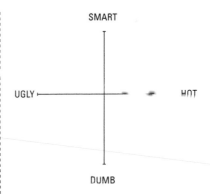

After determining which quadrant she's in, you'll need to create a persona that fits. Here are some examples:

Hot/Dumb

To impress her, tell her you have a job that pays a lot (she's going to have to rely on someone). Show her that you're smarter than her, but don't intimidate her. Make sure to smile a lot and laugh at every stupid thing she says.

EXAMPLES OF HOT/DUMB INCLUDE:

- Paris Hilton
- Jessica Simpson
- Carmen Electra

Ugly/Dumb

Tell her whatever you want. It doesn't matter anyway. She's just grateful you're talking to her.

EXAMPLES OF UGLY/DUMB INCLUDE:

- There are no Ugly/Dumb celebrities. Hollywood has some standards.
- Wait . . . Sarah Jessica Parker.

Hot/Smart

To impress her, you'll have to tread carefully. She's no dummy, so don't tell her you're an astronaut if she works for NASA. Make sure all your lies are in areas she's not too familiar with. She can't know everything.

EXAMPLES OF HOT/SMART INCLUDE:

- Sharon Stone
- Cate Blanchett
- George Clooney

Ugly/Smart

These are the keepers. This is wife material, so don't mess this up. Ugly/Smart women will take care of *you* instead of running off with the gardener—no matter what. After all, what hot young gardener would have her?

EXAMPLES OF UGLY/SMART INCLUDE:

- Barbra Streisand
- Whoopi Goldberg
- Hillary Clinton

25. You're Too Short to Be Noticed by Girls

If you're 6' or taller, this entry isn't for you—unless you happen to be visiting the Netherlands. This fun-loving nation of giants boasts an average male height of 6'1", compared to 5'10" for American males. The reason? Our scientific theory goes like this:

Marijuana use ☞ the "munchies" = food consumption = growth

Others point to a high dairy diet and a relatively even distribution of wealth, leading us to a new, less scientific theory about the benefits of Gouda and socialism. However, some critics argue the experiment was conducted unfairly, with many Dutchman measured while still wearing their clogs.

Nevertheless, if you've been passed over for being too short, or been shot down because you didn't meet her height requirement, and you need some help holding your own in a bar full of giants—in Holland or in your hometown— here are some ways to stand out from the crowd (clogs are optional).

The WTF Approach to Being F*#!-ing Vertically Challenged

➤ **OPTION #1: *Disco Fever***

In case you haven't noticed, the '70s have been back for a while. Shag haircuts and tight jeans could be just the beginning. Be the first person to bring back platform shoes for men . . . *please*!

➤ **OPTION #2: *Be Really Tough and Good Looking***

Go to the gym and get ripped and, if necessary, get plastic surgery. If you look really, really good, women might notice you amongst the giants—particularly if you shove a few of those big shots out of your way!

➤ **OPTION #3: *Inconspicuously Stand on Your Tippy Toes***

This is a great way to catch a lady's attention if you're short—and one of our personal favorites.

Stand by the wall on your tippy toes and rest your heels comfortably on the wall. Instead of being an average-looking short guy, you're now tall and average. The difference is enough to get you laid.

➤ **OPTION #4: *Date Shorter Chicks***

Go out with a tiny girl and you'll feel tall in comparison. Also, your penis will look bigger. Win/win for both parties.

WTFACT: The Danes are the second tallest nation, averaging about 6′ for males. America, which was the tallest nation for many years, now ranks below many Western European nations. Now Europeans can *literally* look down on us.

26. You're Having a Nice Dinner Out but the Waiter Is a Dick

For some of you, complaining to the manager about a nasty, lazy, or just plain stupid waiter comes naturally. But not everyone is born to complain. If you find yourself biting your tongue when you should be standing up for your rights as a customer, follow the WTF Approach instead.

The WTF Approach to Dealing with a F*#!-ing Prick Waiter

➤ **STEP #1: *Remember Who's Boss***

Don't let a snappy attitude or an aura of self-importance alter the dynamic between you and your waiter. Remember that you are in control here—he is here to serve *you*. Think of your waiter as your personal food servant. You wouldn't let a servant tell you what's what, would you? You paid him good money, so you're the boss—act like one.

➤ **STEP #2: *Talk to Him***

At WTF, we're all for diplomacy. If you're having a problem with your waiter, the first thing to do is address him——there's no need to go to his boss right away. If he's being a prick, tell him so. If he takes ten minutes to refill your drink, tell him that what he is doing is unacceptable.

►STEP #3: *Demand the Manager*

If the nasty waiter doesn't change his ways, you need to speak to his manager. This is the point at which you need to shine. Make sure you tell the boss that you "always come here" and that you have "never been treated like this before."

If the manager knows you aren't a regular, you can also say that, "you own five restaurants" and that, "you have never seen anything like this in all your years in the business." This is a good way to embarrass the manager and get the prick waiter fired—plus, it might just mean the difference between a complimentary meal and a $150 check.

Attention All Servants

Lose the f*#!-ing attitude. We don't care whether you work at the fanciest restaurant in Beverly Hills or a stinky diner off Route 66, you are a servant and you should act accordingly. It's your job to serve your customers well and smile wide as you do it.

And yes, it's clear that this is only your "job," not your career. You're a great actor in "real life." But until you actually become the next Daniel Day Lewis, you don't work for MGM—you work for tips. Now go fetch me another goddamn Diet Coke already!

WHAT THE F*#! IS UP WITH . . . BEING AFRAID THEY'RE GOING TO SPIT IN YOUR FOOD

Some people shy away from complaining about bad service because they're scared the waitstaff's going to hock a loogie in their food as an act of revenge. This fear is both cowardly and ridiculous. The chances of this happening are minimal—and near impossible in a quality restaurant. Not to mention that considering the unknown hormones and crap in your two-ton cheeseburger, a little spit should be the least of your concerns.

27. You're in the 10 Items-or-Less Line and the Jerk in Front of You Has 11 Items

If it was a Sunday and you had nothing to do, maybe you would let it slide. But it's a weekday during rush hour and you're just trying to get a few things. You're not in the mood to let some schmuck cut corners—even if he's only trying to sneak in one extra item.

Rules are rules, and this jerk better follow them . . .

The WTF Approach to Getting Some F*#!-ing Grocery Store Justice

➤ STEP #1: *Don't Ever Let Anyone Get Away with It*

Do what it takes. If alerting the grocery bagger doesn't work, demand to speak to a manager. As a last resort, reach into the violator's cart and begin tossing items over your shoulder until only ten items remain. If the violator looks a lot tougher than you, you can also try slamming your shopping cart into his leg. Make sure to get a running start from aisle 5.

WTF: UP CLOSE AND PERSONAL

At WTF, we practice what we preach. One morning before work, I was patiently waiting in the express line at the grocery store to buy bagels for the office (I'm just that kind of guy) when I witnessed someone trying to get away with eleven items instead of the clearly defined maximum of ten. That's right, under a big sign that read "10 Items-or-Less" this rule-breaking anarchist tried to get away scot-free. To be sure, I counted again. Four cans of cat food, two bags of eucalyptus mints, a box of Cream of Wheat, pickled beets, Ovaltine, prune juice, and mint jelly. *Eleven.* So what did I do? I alerted the cashier, of course. I told him of the violation of the store's policy and the following ensued:

"What is he talking about?" the violator said as she turned to me, pretending she didn't know.

ONE WORD OF ADVICE: PLASTIC

Grocery baggers have yet to stop asking customers if they want "paper or plastic?" despite the fact that no one *ever* chooses paper, which is less malleable and harder to carry. Why keep asking? For the *one* person who is so environmentally conscious that she is willing to put up with a little personal inconvenience to help the planet? Ridiculous.

"I'm talking about the fact that the sign says '10 Items or Less' and you have more than the allotted amount, more than what you are permitted to have," I said. "That's cheating, and cheating is wrong."

The cashier just stood there. "Come on, give her a break," said some giant red-haired fool at the back of the line. I turned to him. "Why should I give her a break? Rules are rules."

"She's an old woman."

But why should her age matter? I was not about to let this rule breaker—whatever her age, race,

creed, color, sex, sexual orientation, gender identity, national origin, religion, disability, or familial status—get away with blatant disregard for the rule of law and order. I stood my ground.

"I demand that she goes to another line or forfeits one item of her choice," I commanded. "I want to talk to a supervisor."

It didn't come to that. The rule breaker decided to go to another line, rather than give up one of her items. The cashier and the others in line just stared at me, as if it were *my* fault.

"How could you do that to an old lady?" the red-haired fool repeated.

I just shook my head and laughed. *Old*, I thought. *Yeah, old like a fox.*

—GB

WHAT THE F*#! IS UP WITH . . .
PEOPLE STILL USING CHECKS

Seriously. Unless you're an eighteen year old who just got his first checkbook, writing a check for groceries is embarrassing and takes time. But if you are going to do it, at the very least have the store name, date, and your signature filled out. Don't be surprised, dummy, you always have to put those parts on there. And for those of you who actually ask the cashier who to make the check out to: Well, rack that empty head of yours and take a good f*#!-ing guess!

28. You've Gone to the Bathroom and Realize There's No TP

Many people find going number two to be a very relaxing experience. You can read, think, or practice tele-kinesis—time on the toilet is good clean (well, not *so* clean) fun. Nothing lasts forever, however, and after the deed is done, it's time to clean up and join the rest of the world.

But wait, what if you find that there is nothing there for you to clean up with? And what if you find yourself *alone*—in a house or worse, a public bathroom—without toilet paper? WTF are you going to do? Here are some tips to help guide you through one of the shittiest situations in this book, literally.

The WTF Approach to Being Caught Without F*#!-ing Toilet Paper

> ➤ **OPTION #1:** *Stare at the Holder*

Sometimes staring at the empty holder where toilet paper should be and shaking your head can help you.

> ➤ **OPTION #2:** *Use a Substitute*

First, go to the obvious choice, such as paper towels, which are unfortunately a little out of reach from the toilet in most public

restrooms. That's okay. Hobble there quickly, grab some, and sit back down.

If you aren't lucky enough to have paper towels within a hobble's reach, look to the trashcan. Be careful and exercise caution before taking something out to wipe your ass. Look for used pieces of paper towel, and then smell them to make sure they're wet with water, not urine.

If you can't find paper towels or a trashcan, you're going to have to rough it and use the cardboard toilet paper roll, which is often left on the toilet paper spinner. You might get lucky and there'll even be a little piece of paper stuck to the roll that you can use. Before wiping, make sure to wet half of the cardboard roll in order to make it more malleable, less abrasive, and a more effective shit cleaner. Be sure to keep from running half under the water so you can wipe dry your now-wet ass cheeks. You may also want to break the dry half into smaller pieces so you can go back for a second or third sweep—you don't want to take the chance of wiping your ass in one fell swoop only to find that you're not fully clean—that's just gross.

➤ OPTION #3: *Shower*

If you're in the comfort of your own bathroom, just get your stinky ass up and turn on the shower. Think of it as a giant bidet.

➤ OPTION #4: *Shit Splash*

If you're in a public bathroom, however, and there is no paper or cardboard around, you've got to get creative.

Stand up and waddle to the sink, turn the faucet on warm (but not hot) and, if you're lucky enough to have access to that pink soap, lather up your hands and then turn around.

Next, hop up on the counter and stick your ass right in the sink. This not only brings you closer to the faucet, it prevents any runoff from getting on your underwear and pants that lie on the floor around your ankles.

NOTE: If this is a one-too-many-bean-burrito kind of bathroom trip, you might want to remove your pants and underwear completely before attempting this method of water wiping.

With your ass in the sink, you can now perform the "shit splash" by taking your soapy hand and splashing water between your cheeks. Again, be careful not to spill. You'll still be wet, but with water, not with shit.

➤ OPTION #5:
Call Someone

Cell phones were invented for *just* this type of emergency. Call a friend and get him to bring you some toilet paper.

If you're at someone else's house, it's her fault that you have no toilet paper. So just yell through the door and make her get you some. Who knows, she might feel bad and offer to wipe your ass.

workin' for the man

29. On Your Lunch Break the Soda Machine Eats Your Change

It's your lunch break. The first half of your day's been rough. You're dying for a soda. And if you don't get one, you're liable to scream at your assistant, start smoking again, or even hit the bottle. You slide your buck into the slot, press the button, the machine makes a whole lot of noise, and then . . . nothing comes out. Don't despair, WTF is here.

The WTF Approach to Getting Your F*#!-ing Soda

> **STEP #1:** *Call the Company*

On most vending machines, you'll find a telephone number somewhere near the dollar slot. Call it, and demand that they immediately bring you a soda.

> **STEP #2:** *Call the Cops*

If you walked into a convenience store, grabbed a soda, and walked out, you'd be a thief. If you walked in, gave the guy a dollar and he took the dollar and the soda, he'd be a thief. In this case, the machine is a thief and the authorities must be alerted for the safety of other people whose only crime

was the desire to quench their thirst with, say, a nice refreshing Coke, which is the best cola product on Earth.

> **NOTE:** Coke did not pay for this product placement. But we'll certainly solicit them for our next book.

➤ **STEP #3:** *Get Even*

If no one cares about the machine stealing your money, then they shouldn't care about what you do to it next.

Gather your coworkers and move the soda machine into your office. Leave a note explaining that you'll be happy to return it upon receipt of your hard-earned buck.

TRY OUT THESE NEW DRINKS!

- **Mountain Dick:** With a big dose of caffeine and aphrodisiacs, it won't just keep you up, it will keep your girlfriend up, too.

- **Sprite Lemon:** We took the lime out. It was a huge breakthrough.

- **Frat-paccino:** This drink is a unique blend of Colombian coffee, cocaine, Cheetos, and lukewarm beer.

30. Your New Boss Is Out to Get You

Your new boss is gunning for you and you don't know why. You work hard—or at least you *think* you do. And you're nice to him. So what is his deal? When this happens there is only one thing to do: go over his head. He ain't the King—he's just another putz with a tie. Whether that means to *his* boss, the government, or the IRS, there's always something you can do to let him know that he's not the only one playing for keeps.

The WTF Approach to Beating Your New Boss at His Own F*#!-ing Game

➤ STEP #1: *Look for Dirt*

Check his trash can, his phone log, and if you can, his e-mails. See if he's banging anyone he shouldn't be, if he's embezzling money, or if he's cheating on his taxes. If he's like most of us, he's probably doing *something* wrong.

➤ STEP #2: *Hire a Private Investigator*

If you know his every move, you can get the real dirt. You might be able to blackmail him into letting you become an independent outside advisor, which means you keep your pay and don't work—at least until the board of directors catches on.

➤ STEP #3: *Get Him in Trouble with His Boss*

This is a last resort. File a complaint outlining how he has been harassing you. Feel free to include details about all his shortfalls. In addition, be sure to explain how hesitant you are to do this and how rarely you complain about anything.

Or . . .

➤ STEP #3: *Get the Government Involved*

If your boss is the owner, it may seem like there's no one else to complain to, but there is. Is there an inappropriately placed trash can? Tell OSHA. Are there 1099 workers that should be on payroll? Tell the IRS. And, be sure to let your boss know that you've done so. If he's stupid enough to can you after that, it's considered retaliation for "whistleblowing," which isn't a legal reason to fire someone.

IN THE FUTURE . . .

Be your own boss. Start your own business so you never have to deal with a boss again. If you aren't talented enough to be successful, become a consultant, because if you're incapable of being part of a solution, you can always make money prolonging a problem.

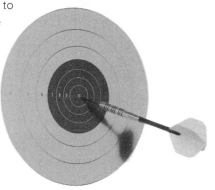

31. A New Coworker Is Driving You Insane

Just as there are different strains of the flu, there are different types of annoying coworkers. You'll find the ass kissers, the sloths, the bullies, and the know-it-alls. But whichever kind of annoying coworker you face, there's one thing you, sadly, can't do—throw him out the f*#!-ing window.

You've been trucking along at your job for a while now, and on a good day enjoy your work. Well, as much as anyone can enjoy work. But this new disease is driving you nuts. He's incompetent, annoying, and his repulsive hyena-pitched laugh bounces off the office walls. You just can't take it anymore. Here's what to do:

The WTF Approach to Handling a Toxic F*#!-ing Coworker

➤ STEP #1: *Make Concessions*

The first thing you must do is try to accommodate his annoying habit by making slight adjustments to your rituals that won't upset your well-being. If the jerk smacks

gum, put on headphones, or steal his pack when he isn't looking.

➤ STEP #2: *Befriend Him to Change Him*

If you're friendly, you might be able to get him to change to be more cool and less annoying. Then again it's not easy to make someone change. Your ex-girlfriend tried that with you, remember?

➤ STEP #3: *If You Can't Beat Him, Join Him*

If that doesn't work, try to do exactly what he's doing. If he's skating by without doing a shred of work because he's a kiss ass, become one too. It's going to take some practice to get it right. The first couple of times you complement your boss on his new suit, he'll probably raise an eyebrow and think you're being sarcastic. But keep

at it. It's about time you put those four college drama classes to use.

➤ STEP #4: *Get His Ass Fired*

If nothing works with this prick, it's time to get serious. Get him fired. A little, innocent sabotage goes a long way. Leaving illegal drugs on his desk or rerouting his home page to a porn site might do the trick.

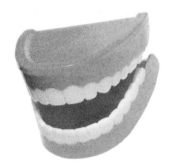

32. You're Out of Personal Days, but Have Tickets to Opening Day

" **Y**ou can't use sick days for non-health-related issues," says your goody-two-shoes coworker. No shit—being at the park for the first pitch of the season is a matter of life or death. Just call in sick and follow these rules.

The WTF Approach to Getting Out of F*#!-ing Work

> **STEP #1:** *Lie*

No matter how cool your boss is, how cool you think he is, or how much you've talked ball with him in the past, *never* tell him the truth about those box seats. *Always* lie. See Options #1 and #2 for possible excuses.

> **OPTION #1:** *Call in Sick*

The truth is that you *are* sick. Or would be if you missed this opportunity. Every kind of sickness can only get worse. And that's why you call out, in order to make sure you get better and not worse and not miss more work. If you have a cold, you call out and stay home from work to avoid turning it into pneumonia. If you have opening day tickets, you call out and go to the game to avoid sinking into a deep depression after you find out you could've been at the game where your team rallied in the bottom of the ninth with a bases-loaded, two out, 3-2 count grand slam.

►OPTION #2: *Other Lies*

If you've been "sick" too often and you don't want to arouse suspicion, come up with a more clever excuse, like:

- You woke up to find a horse's head in your bed.

- You had to answer some tough questions by some nasty Spanish priests.

- You woke up to find that you had turned into an insect.

Making Bad Lies Good

There is a whole list of standard excuses people use such as:

1. Got the flu

2. Grandmother passed away

3. Car broke down/won't start

On the surface, these are typical lies that should be avoided. But, with a little bit of tweaking, they're okay. The trick is to make your excuse both specific and more grandiose.

The previous list of common lies should be converted to these:

1. **Got AIDS.** Instead of the common flu, you now have a fatal disease. This is a good lie for two reasons. First, due to the stigma that still unfortunately surrounds the disease, your boss would *never* think anyone would lie about something like that. Second, and on a related point, it is that very social stigma that would scare your boss into giving you not only the benefit of the doubt in the future, but also special treatment, for fear of some kind of legal action. Finally, having AIDS gives you a green light to use the "flu excuse" whenever you want. After all, you've got to be extra careful not to get *really* sick.

2. **Mom died.** Almost every adult has dealt with the death of a grandmother. No big deal. That's why the "grandmother died" excuse is all too common. But if you say that your mom died instead, you have one of the best excuses for missing work or anything else in the world. You get immediately credibility. After all, what kind of a sick f*#! would lie about his mom dying?

3. **Car is possessed.** Having your car break down is not enough. Getting to work is *your* responsibility, not your boss's. Also, if you say you were in a wreck, you're going to have to show proof that your car was hit. It's best to avoid any excuse relating to your automobile. However, if you're bent on using an auto-related excuse, say that your car, nicknamed "Carrie," has become possessed and is terrorizing the neighborhood. If you say it convincingly, the boss might not believe you, but he will think that you're insane and need treatment. Again, fear of legal action will prevent him from firing you over your mental illness. He'll probably just encourage you to get professional help, which, quite frankly, you might need.

33. Your Computer Crashes and You Lose Your Big Presentation

This is the big one, the one that can take your career to the next level. The one that can get you out of your cubicle and into the corner office. But your computer decided to get an e-STD and shit out on you the night before the big day—losing everything. Maybe it was the spam, maybe it was a virus, or maybe it was all the porn. Don't worry, though, there's always a way to scoot by.

The WTF Approach to Handling a Ruined F*#!-ing Presentation

➤ **OPTION #1: *Rear-End Someone on the Highway***

Pretend you have whiplash, and take a ride in an ambulance to the hospital. Have a nurse leave a message with your boss.

➤ **OPTION #2: *Call in a Bomb Threat***

The good old "bomb in the building" trick always wastes an hour or two. The federal government sees this gag as actual terrorism, so either don't do it or don't get caught.

➤ OPTION #3: *Make Yourself Sick*

First, eat about five hotdogs with lots of ketchup. Then go to your boss's office before the meeting and let him know that you're feeling sick. He'll probably suggest you try to give the presentation anyway. Right before you enter the boardroom, take a swig of ipecac syrup. When the urge to puke hits you, don't resist. Try to make eye contact with him, open your mouth, and let it go. Your colleagues may hate you, but at least you can sue if you're fired.

➤ OPTION #4: *Wing It*

You're never going to make it in the corporate world by wimping out. Computer issues or not, go balls to the wall and do what you do best—bullshit. Here are some things to mention if you decide to wing it:

- Say "synergy" a lot. Just throw the word in wherever. Everyone thinks it's an important concept, even though no one fully understands what it means.

- Talk about the need to increase profit margins and marketshare. Companies like these things.

- Always end with your future plans to enter the Chinese market.

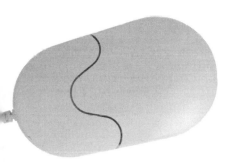

34. Your Ugly Boss Wants to Jump Your Bones

You've caught her staring at your ass. She's bumped against you in the elevator. She calls you into her office just to hand you junk mail. She repeatedly asks to meet outside the office to discuss upcoming projects. Basically, she wants to f*#!.

The WTF Approach to Handling Your F*#!-ing Ugly Boss

➤ OPTION #1: *Get Drunk and Do It*

You'll f*#! anything after a couple of drinks, so why not someone who can better your career? After all, the reason you have a job is to make money so you can get with girls. By getting with this one, you're setting yourself up for even more money, more sex, and more drama—just the way you like it.

➤ OPTION #2: *Bring a Horny Friend*

It might not be you. Your boss might just be hard up. Throw your friend at her to solve the problem. This tactic also gives you an excuse next time she hits on you. Just say you don't date people your friends have dated.

➤ OPTION #3: *Sue Her Ass*

If she crosses the line, sue her. If she hasn't yet, provoke her by wearing tighter pants.

for the ladies . . .

I'll give you the same advice I gave the guys: Close your eyes and do it. You've shagged nastier guys for no good reason. Comparatively, doing it for a promotion is a step up.

UGLY SCALE		BONUS TO MAKE IT WORTH IT
Rosie O'Donnell ➜	10	$5.12 million
Barbara Walters ➜	9	$2.56 million
Heather Mills ➜	8	$1.28 million
Brooke Hogan ➜	7	$640,000
Janice Dickenson ➜	6	$320,000
Kathy Griffin ➜	5	$160,000
Fergie ➜	4	$80,000
Madonna ➜	3	$40,000
Lauren Conrad ➜	2	$20,000
Jessica Biel ➜	1	$10,000

35. You Blew the Company Softball Game

It's the bottom of the ninth. The bases are loaded. You're down by one. All you have to do is get a hit and your office team will win. You'll be the hero, and coworkers will tell stories about you at the water cooler until next year's big game. Strike one. Strike two. Strike three. You're a f*#!-ing loser. Now what?

The WTF Approach to Not F*#!-ing Blowing It

➤ STEP #1: *Convert*

Your God just isn't working out for you.
Try another one.

➤ STEP #2: *Practice for Next Year's Game*

Practice may not make perfect, but it might save you from being the office schmuck. Learn how to get a f*#!-ing grip: Hold the bat like a bat, not like a dick.

➤ STEP #3: *Sit It Out*

In key situations, ask to sit on the bench. If you need to fake an injury, do it. You'll never be the hero, but anything's better than being the villain.

➤ STEP #4: *Change Jobs*

If finding another job in the United States doesn't create enough distance between you and your folly, get a job in China. They like ping pong anyway.

IN THE FUTURE . . .

Fake a seizure. If there's a chance you're going to screw up in a key situation, start twitching and fake a seizure. People will assume that a malady of some sort caused it. By the time the ambulance shows up, they'll pray for God to save your life, not to take it. This way, you'll never have a chance to mess up in the first place. This tactic will also work if you are about to screw up an important presentation or even if you're late for work.

36. You're Taking a Business Trip and Your Wife Wants to Go

One of the few perks of corporate life is occasionally getting to travel. While St. Louis might not be Paris, at least it enables you to take a break from the stress of domestic responsibility and enjoy a little time for yourself. But what if that domestic stress travels with you? Here's how to make sure your wife doesn't want to come along.

The WTF Approach to Ditching the F*#!-ing Mrs.

➤ **STEP #1:** *Lie About Where You're Going*

Tell your wife you are going to places that she would never want to go. Dangerous places are the best. If you are taking an international trip, tell her you're going to Iraq. If you are taking a domestic trip, tell her you are going to Detroit. In fact, no matter where you are going, always say Detroit.

➤ **STEP #2:** *Induce a Terrible Fear of Flying*

Make her scared of flying. In the weeks before your trip, bring up any news story that has to do with plane crashes (or just make some shit up). You can also start watching movies that will freak her out about flying, like *Airport*, *Alive*, *Fearless*, or *Die Hard 2*, and make sure she's really on edge.

➤ STEP #3: *Bore the Shit Out of Her*

Tell her every single detail of your trip, including all the meetings you'll be going to and the characteristics of all the boring people who will be there. Most important, go over your boring presentation a thousand times. Just think about all the boring things you normally tell her about your work and multiply it by a factor of 10.

37. Your Assistant Is Making a Play for Your Job

Sometimes ambitious coworkers get a little *too* ambitious and want to move up at your expense. While getting them fired might be an option, it's not always the best choice for your department or the company. And besides, there are other ways to deal with this delicate situation. Of course, you could just do your job well. If you're on top of your game, you won't have to worry about being replaced. Nah, follow these rules instead.

The WTF Approach to Squashing a F*#!-ing Underling

➤ STEP #1: *Put Him in His Place*

Make a clear distinction between who's the boss and who's not. This should help to keep the usurper in his place.

➤ STEP #2: *No Exceptions*

Don't let him park in a manager's space, even when he comes in for overtime work on Christmas Day. Those spots are for managers, not assistants. Rules apply 24/7, 365 days a year.

➤ STEP #3: *Don't Socialize*

Don't fraternize with him outside the office. He's your bitch, not your buddy.

➤ STEP #4: *Put Him Down*

If he makes a mistake, let him—along with the rest of the office, his girlfriend, and his mom—know.

➤ STEP #5: *Keep It Formal*

Don't let him call you by your first name. You're "Sir," "Boss," or "Master."

➤ STEP #6: *Humble Him*

Whenever you have an important visitor, call him in to take your lunch order.

➤ STEP #7: *Take Away His Toys*

Replace his Mac with an Etch-a-Sketch and demand the same quality work.

When It's Serious

If it's gotten to the point where it's either you or him and you suspect the big bosses might choose him, do whatever it takes to get him out of there, including:

- Plant drugs in his office and call the feds.

- Masturbate on his desk. Make sure that you haven't jerked off in a few days so you can get as much as possible on his possessions

- Change his home page from Yahoo.com to Blowjob.com.

- Slash his tires every morning, and complain that he's always late.

- Put rotten food and insects in his desk drawer.

- Have sex with his wife (just because).

dealing with money trouble

38. You Overdraw Your Account by 25¢ and Get Charged $25

Most banks like nothing more than to kick you when you're down. When you cut it close, they're just waiting for you to make the slightest miscalculation so they can charge you twenty-five bucks. This is particularly irritating when you put a sandwich on your card, add a tip, and get nailed twenty-five bucks for each charge. The grand total for the sandwich is now $56. And you thought it was a waste at six bucks. In cases like this, there's only one thing to do:

The WTF Approach to F*#!-ing Overdrafting

The best way to handle this situation is by *rep surfing*. Rep surfing is when you call customer service until you get a rep who gives in to your demands. With a click of a button, a rep can save you a load of cash by bending the rules a tiny little bit. Follow these steps:

> ►STEP #1: *Call in the Middle of the Night*

If the rep ain't got shit to do, he might hear you out.

> ►STEP #2: *Give Him a Sob Story*

Gain the service rep's sympathy and he'll be putty in your hands.

➤ STEP #3: *Remember—It's Not His Fault*

Even though you want to tell him he's a dipshit, don't. He's not the one fining you; it's the bank.

➤ STEP #4: *Remind Him of Your Loyalty*

Don't let him forget how many years you've been a customer of the bank. While the rep certainly doesn't give a shit, it'll make it easier for him to get away with.

➤ STEP #5: *Ask What He Can Do*

Now that you've reminded him of your customer loyalty, ask him nicely if he can do anything for you. This makes losers like him feel special and powerful, and he just might bend company policy to help you out.

NOTE: The lunatic method in which you start screaming and carrying on works best at a branch office. But word to the wise—keep an eye on the security guard.

39. Your Ex Charges Up Your Credit Cards as a Goodbye Present

It's easy to overspend with a credit card—and even easier for a bitter ex. Unless you're Larry King and can easily pay an ex-wife's spiteful shopping spree, you're liable to pay up the hefty sum.

The WTF Approach to Dealing with F*#!-ing Debt

➤ STEP #1: *Blame Her*

Not that the card company will care about your bitter battle. As long as she had authorization to use your card before her meltdown, you're liable for her charges. The chance of this happening is almost worth not just tossing your next girl the plastic when she begs you to go shopping with her.

➤ STEP #2: *Max Out Your Cards*

Chances are your sob story isn't going to work. So if you're already screwed with your credit card company and don't see any light at the end of the tunnel, royally screw yourself. F*#! it. Go out and have a good time.

➤ STEP #3: *Disappear*

Change your address. Change your phone number. Change your name. They're going to try to hunt you down after you've maxed out your cards. You have to be ready to run *Fugitive*-style. But instead of hunting down your wife's killer, you might consider hunting down your credit card charging ex and killing her.

Welcome to the Real World

When someone lends you money, the reason they charge you high interest is because of the risk involved. For the credit card companies, they're making an investment in you, which didn't pay off. That's life. A world where every investment paid off would be a perfect one: one where violence, drugs, and sexually transmitted diseases didn't exist. But we don't live in that world. We live in a WTF kind of world. A world where you find a field of pot growing in your backyard, a world where your home gets infested with termites, and a world where your favorite television show is cancelled. In this world, not every investment pays off.

Credit Contracts

You obviously have never read a credit card contract, or else you wouldn't have a credit card. You may be surprised that being able to jack up your interest rate at will is just the beginning. If you miss a payment the credit card company can:

- Turn your guest room into a collection call center.

- Take your kids on that trip to Disney World you've been promising them for years but couldn't because you've been neck-deep in credit card debt. Why would they do this? Because credit card companies are vicious, mean, and have an appreciation of the ironic.

- Nail your wife.

40. You're at the Grocery Store but Forgot Your Wallet

Stealing is wrong. While few will debate this cornerstone of civilization, there is a grey area. *Sometimes* stealing is acceptable—like when you're starving and left your wallet at home. While in some countries they lop off your hand if you're caught stealing, in America we'll probably give you a slap across the wrists. So if you need to bend the rules to fill your stomach, there are guidelines to save yourself from a wrist-slapping—or hand-chopping as the case may be.

The WTF Approach to Feeding Your Face without a F*#!-ing Dime

➤ STEP #1: *Clear that Conscience*

Nothing says, "I'm guilty" more than a guilty conscience.

➤ STEP #2: *Clean Yourself Up*

If you look like a vagrant, they'll be watching you. Then again, if you didn't look like a vagrant, you wouldn't be stealing food.

➤ STEP #3: *Keep It Cheap*

Don't steal high-priced items like lox, caviar, or truffles. Steal bread, hotdogs, or SPAM.

NOTE: Stay away from the liquor. We know you're thirsty, but go out and earn that shit by begging like every other dumb drunk.

> ➤ STEP #4: *Don't Worry about Getting Caught*

The cops will feed you in the jail house, and if you've been reduced to stealing hot dogs, you probably don't have anywhere better to be.

Scam Time

If you're adept at lying, you might be able to skip the stealing and go right to scamming your way to a decent meal. If you think you're up to it, try one of these:

The Fast Food Scam: Don't tell anyone we told you this, but fast-food restaurants are easy to scam. Grab a bag with their logo on it out of the trash from their parking lot. Pick one or two items that you'd like to eat. Now, drive up to the window and tell them they forgot to put those items in your bag. Tell them that you were there just thirty minutes ago and that it was a big order, so they must remember. They'll likely fork those items over no questions asked. If they do ask you anything, just come up with a believable story. If a fast-food worker can catch you in a lie, it may be better that you starve.

The Grocery Store Scam: In a grocery store parking lot there are receipts galore. Pick one up, and choose the food of your choice from the list. Go inside and complain that the item wasn't included. Be sure to ask for a manager and act confident. This will not work with a Thanksgiving Day Turkey or a watermelon.

The Pizza Scam: Order a pizza with a bunch of toppings. When the delivery arrives, check the pizza and immediately complain that it's missing a topping. Call up the shop and speak to the manager and complain. Tell him that you will not pay for it because it's not the pizza you ordered. If he offers to send another one, tell him to forget it because you're starving. They might take the pizza back, but they'll probably leave it for you. If it doesn't work, try another pizza shop.

41. Your Roommate Skips Out the Day Before Rent Is Due

It's the first of the month and, as usual, you can barely come up with your half of the rent—let alone your roomie's half. You had a feeling that you couldn't trust that guy. Shit! You can try to reason with your landlord, but he is probably a heartless bastard. So, what can you do? In pornographic movies, the landlord takes sex as payment for rent. In the real world, this is less common. Sure, your landlord may want to tap that ass, but he's got bills, too.

Still, there's always something that can be done when it's the first of the month and you're short on funds, and with WTF, you might just be able to keep a roof over your head.

The WTF Approach to Making Your F*#!-ing Rent

► OPTION #1: *Sell Your Junk*

You can probably sell a lot of things lying around your apartment. CDs, DVDs, and video games should be sold off first. If you're really short, start selling jewelry and appliances. Hit up eBay or similar auction sites to hock your wares, but avoid pawnshops, since they give you a bad

rate, and you'll never come up with the money to get your stuff back anyway.

➤ OPTION #2: *Sell Your Body*

If you're decent looking and have lax morals, get a job at a strip club. If you're not so cute, get a job at a shitty strip club. You can also go on craigslist and sell whatever services you have to offer, even if they don't seem like much. Willing to give nude massages, light spankings, or let strangers take a dump on your stomach? There's a market for your services.

➤ OPTION #3: *Sell Your Children*

When worse comes to worst, you can sell off your children to science, the circus, or possibly a high-profile celebrity with an adoption addiction—think Angelina Jolie. At least these people will be able to afford to keep a roof over your kids' heads.

➤ OPTION #4: *Borrow Money*

If you haven't already used up your credit line with your friends and family, go ahead and borrow a little from them. They know you're not good for it, so don't feel too bad about not paying them back.

If everyone in your personal life knows what a no-good slacker you are and won't float you a few bucks, max out your credit cards, get a couple payday loans, take whatever credit any moron will give you, and then change your phone number. Don't borrow from the mob, though—you'll end up renting a hospital bed or spot in the nearest river if you do.

➤ OPTION #5: *Get a New Roommate*

So what if you think you prefer to live alone. You'd also prefer to fly first class, drive a Mercedes, and spend your summers in the Hamptons, but you can't even make your rent. Just think of it as college,

except you're thirty. If you're a post grad at your local university, choose wisely; your new roomie might have tons of sexy, co-ed friends that love older guys.

➤ OPTION #6: *Change the Locks*

Buy some time before they break down the door. In the meantime, try to come up with the cash or start packing. If you can't move in with your parents and have no friends, find a codependent lover to move in with.

➤ OPTION #7: *Move*

You could always follow the lead of your prick roommate and bounce before your landlord has a chance to evict you. Granted, your new living arrangements will be a little different from your current situation.

Old Place:

1200sf home, 2BR 2BA, with a big backyard shaded by two huge beautiful maple trees. Gleaming hardwood floors, spacious kitchen with huge range/oven and updated cabinets, fireplace, central heating and air conditioning. Very large living room with big windows looking out on the great backyard. Each bedroom has its own full bath.

New Place:

Chevy Blazer, '87, 2 door, V6, power windows, 4 x 4, clean interior, clean engine, runs good, stereo, A/C needs to be recharged.

42. You Got Laid Off and Now You're Broke

In this economy, every paycheck could be your last. If you find yourself out of work, out of cash, and out of luck, you can try these options.

The WTF Approach to Living without a F*#!-ing Income

> **OPTION #1: *Beg for Money***

A classic way of obtaining cash for drugs is begging for change on the street. This is a difficult game, however, and with so much competition out there (you're not the only loser, you know) you've got to get creative to survive. Here are some great ideas for panhandling angles:

- **Be Specific.** The key to any good sympathetic story is specificity. Be specific about how much you need. Ask for a quarter to use a payphone or $1.50 to catch the bus. The more money, the more specific you need to be.

- **Be a Fish-Out-of-Water.** Everyone loves a story about a fish out of water. Think of Jon Voight down on his luck in the Big Apple in *Midnight Cowboy*. If you're doing the "I'm stranded and I want to go back home to my nice dumb town" routine,

again ask for something specific, like $17 for a greyhound ticket. This is a lot of money for panhandling, but if you come across the right kind of compassionate fool, you just might succeed.

- **Be Crippled.** If you are crippled, that's great for panhandling, though admittedly not great for much else. If you're not, do the old Eddie Murphy no legs routine from *Trading Places*. Who knows, you might be living like a fat cat in no time.

- **Be a Vet.** If you actually are a vet, good for you, and we humbly thank you for your service. Now get the f*#! off the street! If you aren't a vet, hit up the Army Surplus store and invest in your future.

- **Be Earnest.** Some beggars choose to be blatantly honest, betting on people's appreciation of the truth and sense of

humor to make them give. Put up a sign that reads something like "Fired by The Man" or "The Economy Sucks" and see how people respond.

➤ OPTION #2: *Steal*

Stealing is a classic way to get quick cash. Now, while we don't condone stealing, if you are going down this road anyway, at least steal from corporations rather than directly from individuals. It's simply not as bad to steal a watch from Bloomingdales as it is to steal the neighbor kid's brand new red bicycle. Though, it might make a good getaway vehicle if you don't already have one.

➤ OPTION #3: *Sell Yourself*

Becoming a prostitute is also a great way to earn quick cash. If you're any good at it, you just found yourself employed in a recession-proof profession.

43. You Owe a Lot of Money to the IRS

First of all, while it might seem cool to owe money to bad guys—all that danger, intrigue, and other bullshit—we're talking the IRS here. They make Tony Soprano look like a pussy. Bad guys can threaten you with a swim in the East River. The IRS promises poverty, humiliation, and a trip up the river. Here are tips for when Uncle Sam's cronies come knocking.

The WTF Approach to Handling a Debt with the F*#!-ing Government

➤ OPTION #1: *Pay 'Em*

Don't be a cheapskate. If you've got the dough, cough it up. It's better to be broke than to be locked up. Well, unless you're *really* broke.

➤ OPTION #2: *Grow a Beard and Work Out*

This is a great way to naturally disguise your appearance while you plan a potential getaway. If you don't have this kind of time before the IRS comes looking for you, try the old Groucho Marx nose and glasses routine. Fair warning: These guys are not as dumb as you think.

➤ OPTION #3: *Move*

Sometimes just leaving town is enough to keep you safe. At least for a little while. Just remember to learn your lesson and pay your f*#!-ing taxes. If you don't learn your lesson, you'll run out of places to hide. And they will find you, sooner or later.

➤ OPTION #4: *Gamble For Your Freedom*

Take your last few coins to the casino and go for it. Maybe you'll win big enough to pay off your debt. Maybe you'll lose it all. The little cash you have left won't matter much when you're your cellmate's bitch.

Geographical Hierarchy of "Bad" Guys

There are bad guys all over the world. But here's a breakdown of where most can be found—or better yet, avoided.

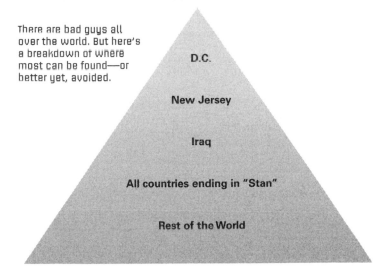

D.C.

New Jersey

Iraq

All countries ending in "Stan"

Rest of the World

44. Your Stock Portfolio Takes a Sudden Dive

You wake up in the morning, grab a bagel and an orange juice, and read the paper. It's your usual routine, checking the *Wall Street Journal* to see your stocks and those little plus signs next to the company you invested in so heavily. All's well—nothing can keep you from riches that will soon be pouring in. Then you turn on the television to find that every channel is breaking in with the report that the company's bankrupt and your stocks are in the dumps. It's over—no more little plus signs.

The WTF Approach to F*#!-ing Sunken Stocks

➤ STEP #1: *Sell Your Hummer*

This was the first thing you bought when your stocks started to soar. We know, it looks cool—but you're poor now and can't afford the gas. If driving a tank compensated for your small penis, we'd say keep it. But it doesn't.

➤ STEP #2: *Start Suing*

Go after everyone you can think of, for reasons that don't even have to really make sense, and see what sticks. It's the American way.

➤ STEP #3: *Get Back to Work*

Early retirement was boring, anyway. Did you really want to sell your condo in New Jersey and travel on a luxurious yacht?

Or . . .

➤ STEP #3: *Defenestration*

Like they did in the 1920s when people lost fortunes, you could jump out a window. But if you're not above the fourth floor, don't bother. You'll just get another bill.

It's Time to Sell When . . .

Here are some signals that may make you want to dump your position as shareholder.

- Pauly Shore is appointed CEO.

- Your company announces a new drug to cure cancer—but it's in the furniture business.

- The latest earnings conference call was cut short because the company didn't pay the bill.

IN THE FUTURE . . .

Learn your lesson. If you ever get money again, stop investing in speculative stocks because your brother says he knows a guy who knows a guy who says it's going to go up. Pick a safe bet like oil or gold. The dollar will continue to fall forever (generally, making gold more valuable). And don't worry about alternative energy. We won't get serious about that until every last drop of oil is sucked from the earth.

- You call customer service and the CEO answers.

- They're headquartered in Vancouver. Trust us, look it up.

NOTE: WTF is not registered as an investment advisor in any jurisdiction whatsoever—not even Vancouver.

traveling at home and abroad

45. You Have to Spend Your Vacation Fund on a Root Canal

All year, you've been slaving away, saving up, looking forward to the little time your employer gives you off. But when the time finally comes, you're inevitably short on cash.

Now, you could always just do nothing. Who really cares about Mount Rushmore, Machu Picchu, or the French? The world is full of boring shit, bugs, and disease, and by staying home, you'll have plenty of time to catch up on daytime television, those books you bought in the '90s, and masturbating.

But if you really need a getaway and don't have any loot, here's what to do.

The WTF Approach to F*#!-ing Vacationing on the Cheap

➤ **OPTION #1: *Turn Your Apartment into an Exotic Locale***

Get blowup palm trees and some margarita mix, toss some dirt on the floor, and hang a crucifix on the wall. Now you could be in one of dozens of Latin American countries. If you live in L.A., just go outside for the same effect. Also, tell your colleagues you're going somewhere exotic to do something you like to do, for example:

Alaska for fishing, Australia for surfing, or Cambodia for sex with prepubescent girls. While you're holed up at home, be sure to read up on your supposed destination, including travel memoirs of people who aren't losers and could afford to actually go. This material will give you stories to share once your vacation ends and everyone asks you about your trip.

> ➤ **OPTION #2:** *Charge It*

If you haven't yet loaded up all your credit cards, you're one of the few Americans who can still charge it. Join the crowd, load up your cards, and worry about it when you get home. Be sure to get some of those pricey cash advances because in the Third World, whether that is New Delhi or New Orleans, they only take cash.

> ➤ **OPTION #3:** *Travel on the Cheap*

Stay local instead of going to some distant place. Sleep in your car or a tent instead of a hotel. Eat at Taco Bell instead of the Cheesecake Factory. Pick up women with your good looks and charm instead of hiring hookers.

You can also try to hop a freighter ship. While it might be slightly less comfortable than a cruise, at least the deck won't be swarming with boozed-up retirees.

Top Travel Destinations for Losers and Cheapskates

Las Vegas: Flights there are relatively cheap and there's always a hotel deal somewhere. If you stay away from gambling, strippers, and shows, Vegas can be a bargain. But if you stay away from gambling, strippers, and shows, why the hell would you go to the desert?

Camp Anywhere: Without exception, every place in America is only an hour or two from some kind of mediocre nature park. Also without exception, every person in America has a buddy who owns a tent he bought when trying to shag some dirty hippie.

Mexico: About 25 percent of Americans live less than a day's drive from Mexico. Go there. Avoid pricey tourist traps and you'll feel like a king. Plus, you can bring back pharmaceuticals, cheap tequila, or even Mexicans to finance your trip. You should focus on the pharmaceuticals, however, as they are easier to carry and fetch a far higher price.

HOW PEOPLE SPEND VACATION	
Having fun:	5%
Trying to have fun:	10%
Hung over from trying to have fun:	15%
Worrying about having fun:	70%

46. You're Lost Abroad and Need to Find the Train Station

First of all, what the f*#! are you doing in Timbuktu? And why can't they speak English? It's not your fault *at all* that you're traveling around unprepared and uneducated, now lost and without the slightest idea of how to get to the train station for your 11:30 departure. Weren't the British bringing civilization, the English language, and tea to every corner of the world? Well, they were, but the Spanish and French were out there, too—and they had better food. But now you're lost with your thumb up your ass like some dumb American.

The WTF Approach to Not Knowing the F*#!-ing Language

> ➤ **OPTION #1:** *Find a Translator*

Your best bet is to hire a local or make a local language–speaking friend. There's always some hot, desperate, English-speaking NGO moron trying to save the world. Ask her.

> ➤ **OPTION #2:** *Gesture*

You should be able to use universal gestures for basic directions. Find a local who looks like he can handle a rousing game of charades. Raise both hands and shrug to signal you have a question.

Then try to simulate a movement or two that will relate you're looking for a train station. Maybe break out a few moves from the opening of *Soul Train.* You'll either end up getting to the station or in some underground club with flashing lights, lots of bass, and a smoke machine. Either way, you win.

> **NOTE:** If you're lost in an oppressive country, be careful asking for help using hand gestures; one wrong move could be fatal. In some countries, they'll not only respond by moving their index finger across their neck to simulate cutting your throat—they'll actually do it.

➤ OPTION #3: *Go to an Irish Pub*

There's one in every corner of the world. Ask for Seamus. He'll either give you directions to the station, or get you drunk enough not to care where you are.

➤ OPTION #4: *Enjoy Yourself*

Forget about getting home. Immerse yourself in the culture. Who knows, you just might find it more interesting than Cleveland. *Hmm,* maybe not.

Traveling Checklist for Visiting Another Country

Before you head out, save yourself some trouble and ask yourself these questions about your intended destination:

❑ Has the civil war calmed down?

❑ Can you go without getting a vaccination?

❑ Can you walk around at night without a police escort?

❑ Can you find a good piece of cheesecake?

❑ Are they still lenient regarding prostitution (not that you're interested or anything, you just prefer liberal governments)?

❑ Can you actually speak the f^#!-ing language?

If you did not answer yes to all of the above questions, go to Florida . . . again.

47. You're Arrested in the Third World for No Good Reason

You thought you were obeying the rules, but maybe you should have done a little more research about what was legal and what wasn't before you traveled to your Third World destination. You might have found out that many of these shit holes share one law in common: A law that makes it illegal to be white and look like you have money. Of course, they'll say they pulled you over for speeding on your motorbike, but really they just want to shake you down for a few bucks.

While going to jail in the United States isn't a walk in the park, being locked up in Laos will make a stint in Rikers Island feel like a day at the beach. Trust us. Now, we're not going to lie to you. In this situation, even with WTF, you're pretty much f*#!-ed.

The WTF Approach to Surviving a F*#!-ing Third-World Jail

➤ STEP #1: *Get Used to Eating Rodents and Insects*

They'll be running around everywhere, and they taste better and are more nutritious than the shit they'll feed you.

➤ STEP #2: *Convert*

Start believing whatever religion they believe in. Everyone loves a convict that turned to God, as long as it's their God.

➤ STEP #3: *Try to Avoid Drinking the Water*

Until it dries up, drink your own piss. Do not drink piss from other inmates, however tempting. Even the water is better than that.

➤ STEP #4: *Don't Get F*#!-ed in the Ass*

Just like at home, you don't want to get f*#!-ed in the ass by a prisoner. Sure, it may hurt less in Bangkok than in Pelican Bay, but the chances of getting AIDS are moderately higher.

➤ STEP #5: *Bribe Them*

The good thing about a corrupt system is that it's corrupt. They may put you away for twenty years for stealing a pack of gum, but they also might take $20 to let you go on a homicide charge. Pay up and get out.

48. A Hurricane Ruins Your Honeymoon

>>>>>> You survived the wedding, the family, and bridezilla herself. Now you want to spend a little time on the beach, tanning, recovering, and sipping fruity drinks. But, the ocean doesn't give a shit about your petty problems. It's more interested in evaporation, condensation, and one mother-f*#!-ing monstrous storm.

The WTF Approach to Dealing with a Rainy F*#!-ing Honeymoon

►OPTION #1: *Get Out*

If you're scared of a little water, we don't blame you. Buy the first plane ticket out of town and watch the destruction on CNN from your safe little living room. Expect to pay big bucks for those tickets. The airline has bills to pay, too.

►OPTION #2: *Stay In*

Luckily, it's easy to find cardboard in third-world places like Louisiana, Mexico, and Florida. Tape it to your hotel window, and have your honeymoon where you ought to have it—in the bedroom. Scuba diving, massages, and the beach are all just foreplay anyway.

➤ OPTION #3: *Go Out*

If you can't afford to get out, and the prospect of anymore nookie with bridezilla makes you sick, go surfing. Think Brody from *Point Break.* The good part of this is: you're either stupid and dead or stupid and awesome.

IN THE FUTURE . . .

Don't go to hurricane territory during hurricane season. We know that it was a good deal. That's because it's f*#!-ing hurricane season!

WTF: UP CLOSE AND PERSONAL

Shortly after I was married, my new wife and I honeymooned in Cancun. It happened to be in the middle of hurricane season, but I went online and learned that hurricanes don't go there every year, no big deal. Plus, the airfare and hotel were so cheap that I would have booked it even if it looked like a meteor was going to hit there. The day before the trip, we heard about a hurricane forming. We were kind of excited, a little scared, but after the wedding we needed that goddamn trip. For several days, we watched the monster approach, both on CNN and out the window of the hotel. Then, it turned, destroying Belize. It was kind of disappointing.

—AWH

49. Everyone Else Is Going 90 MPH but You Get Pulled Over

Everybody speeds. That's good for cops. It's their bread and butter. Nabbing a crook is an expense for the state with all the court and jailing costs; nailing someone going ten miles over the limit is easy money. So next time you're minding your business, speeding along with everyone else, and the blue lights start flashing—blame capitalism.

The WTF Approach to Getting Out of a F*#!-ing Ticket

If you get pulled over, don't let the uniform, the boots, and the gun intimidate you. He's not going to shoot you if he catches you in a lie. Instead, remember back to when you were a kid, when lying to authorities was not only no big deal, but good fun, too.

> ➤ **OPTION #1:** *Hospital Emergency*

Say that you were rushing to the hospital. Just don't be cliché. Don't say your wife or your mother is in trouble; that's too standard. Say your mother's cousin or your stepsister. The obscure specificity will lay the groundwork for him to believe you.

➤ OPTION #2: *You Left the Oven On*

While this isn't as emotionally evocative, it can't be disproved with a phone call.

➤ OPTION #3: *You're Late for a Meeting*

This opens up a dialogue between you and the cop, which could lead to him letting you off the hook if you get along. When the cop asks you what you do, don't pick something you know he'll hate or have disdain for, like a stockbroker, a lawyer, or a drug dealer. Say you're something he can either relate to or is universally liked, like a fireman or a doctor.

➤ OPTION #4: *You're About to Crap Your Pants*

With clenched teeth and a grimacing face, explain to the police officer that you have a serious case of colitis and you just finished the world's largest burrito. If you can, let a wet one rip. You'll probably ruin a pair of underwear, but you'll save yourself a ticket. Even Robocop would pity you.

➤ OPTION #5: *You're Being Followed*

Say you're sure you're being chased. Be sure to describe the car's color and model and give one or two numbers in the license plate. There's a fine line between being convincing and sounding like a paranoid lunatic. Depending how well you do, he'll either put out an APB and let your ticket slide, or he'll take you in for suspicion of drug use.

for the ladies . . .

If you're an attractive woman, you don't need a stepsister in the hospital, you don't need to be a firewoman, and you don't even need the threat of soiling yourself. Just smile while you toss your hair. If that doesn't work and you like him, offer to toss his salad, too.

50. A Detour Takes You Through a Bad Part of Town

With all the news and films about violence in America's inner cities, you might be nervous about going through certain parts. But sometimes construction or a car wreck sends you to some very sketchy neighborhoods. Here are some very basic rules you can follow to increase your chances of ever getting out.

The WTF Approach to Taking a F*#!-ing Detour

➤ STEP #1: *Avoid Driving Through at Night*

If the detoured drive can wait until it's light out, wait. While you can get jacked in the daytime, the darkness of night is every criminal's favorite cover.

➤ STEP #2: *Watch What You Wear*

Avoid wearing gang colors. (Red and blues are out.) If you're a guy, don't wear anything that makes you look gay. And if your sunglasses are aviators, take them off—people may take you for a cop, which would be bad news. Your best bet is to get down to boots, jeans, and a T-shirt if possible. If not, good luck.

➤ STEP #3: *Turn Down Your Music*

A car with a nice sound system just screams, "Steal me!" Remember, you're trying *not* to draw attention.

➤ STEP #4: *Don't Make Any Stops*

If you're thirsty, low on gas, or out of smokes, it can probably wait. The only acceptable reason to stop is a red light or a stop sign. Even then, keep your eyes peeled. Better to make an unnecessary right-hand turn than get your car stolen.

Inner Cities Can Be Fun

Inner cities may be dirtier and more dangerous, but they're also more fun. Think of Rio de Janeiro—one of the world's most visited places, but also one of the most dangerous. Danger is fun; getting killed is not. Unfortunately, where there's a lot of danger, fools get shot.

REMEMBERING RODNEY

"I came from a real tough neighborhood. I put my hand in some cement and felt another hand."

—Rodney Dangerfield

IN THE FUTURE . . .

Use the buddy system. Next time you know a detour will be taking you through a shady part of town, talk a friend into going with you. At least then you won't die alone.

---

51. You Need to Go but You Can't Find a Bathroom

It's happened to all of us, even those who have tremendous control over our bodily functions. You're out of your house with no public restrooms in sight, and all of a sudden you've got to piss like a racehorse. Where are you supposed to go? Not just anyplace will do—or will it?

The WTF Approach to Not Having a Bathroom in F*#!-ing Sight

➤ **OPTION #1:** *Go in an Alley*

But be sure not to accidentally piss too close to a bum. If you do, toss him a couple bucks for messing up his crib.

➤ **OPTION #2:** *Hit Up the Gas Station*

They usually have a bathroom, and they're usually lenient about

letting people use it. That's why they're so f*#!-ing filthy.

➤ **OPTION #3:** *Shit in the Street*

If you have to take a shit, hold yourself up between two parked cars for leverage and let it drop. For toilet paper, use foliage, trash, or, if you can't find anything, rub your ass on the side of the vehicle.

➤ OPTION #4: *Pick a Nice Place*

The fancier the restaurant, the more likely they are to let you use the bathroom without eating there. Because they're not inundated with these requests like the less ritzy places, they're likely to make an exception. Unless, of course, you look like a bum. But if you are a bum, you already know where to go. Next stop, the ritzy parking lot.

➤ OPTION #5: *Use Someone's House*

If you're nowhere near home or a friend's house, and you have a phobia about public bathrooms—and you're not about to shit on the street—there's only one option: Put on the necktie you keep in your trunk and impersonate a

Jehovah's Witness. If people don't slam the door on you, kindly ask to use their bathroom. Don't worry, if you get into a conversation about the faith, the only thing you need to remember is that they hate birthdays.

> **IN THE FUTURE . . .**
>
> Always keep a Super Big Gulp cup in your car. They're obviously made to shit in—no one wants that much Mountain Dew.

52. The Person Next to You on the Plane Won't Shut Up

You don't know how it happened, but somehow a couple of cordial hellos turned into his life story. Now the putz won't shut his mouth.

The WTF Approach to Dealing with a Noisy F*#!-ing Seatmate

> **STEP #1: *Avoid Eye Contact***

This should signal that you're not interested in chatting.

> **STEP #2: *Keep It Short***

Answer questions with simple yeses and nos. With luck, he'll take the hint.

> **STEP #3: *Get Busy***

Engage yourself with a book or some paperwork. This tactic might show him that the conversation

is over. If you're dealing with a real pain in the ass, he'll probably ask you about your book or your papers, opening up a whole new can of worms.

> **STEP #4: *Get Up***

Break up the conversation by going to the restroom. No matter how deep you are in conversation, you can always excuse yourself to pee. Bring a blanket when you return to your seat. Close your

eyes and lean back, signaling to him that you're going to sleep.

➤ STEP #5: *Tell Him to Shut Up*

If he still won't shut his trap, tell him that you enjoyed speaking to him, but you really must get some sleep. Say it politely, but make it very clear. This should shut up 99 percent of airplane nuisances.

IN THE FUTURE . . .

Don't forget your iPod— it'll help you block him out.

Or . . .

Take four Tylenol PMs and have a beer before you get on the plane. Worst case, you stay asleep . . . forever.

➤ STEP #6: *Get Serious*

For the 1 percent who are still talking, you'll have to take serious action. Look for an empty seat and move there, unless it's next to a kid or a really fat person. If there isn't an empty seat, tell the flight attendant to find someone to switch seats with you. If there's a noisy kid on the plane without his parents, have him sit in your seat. That way, the two most obnoxious creatures onboard can enjoy each other's company.

➤ STEP #7: *Get Even*

If you can't switch seats, order a cocktail and spill it on him when you hit turbulence. Then order milk and do the same thing. If that doesn't work, order a cup of coffee.

Best New Airline Deals

It's no secret that the airline industry is suffering. These companies will do anything now to get your ass onboard. Some new initiatives:

- If an engine goes out, get a free shitty cabernet.

- Fly ten times a year and get a complimentary pilot's license.

- Take a layover Saturday night and spend it with a flight attendant of your choice.

- If the landing gear doesn't come down, you get a free Salisbury steak.

53. Some Jerk Cuts You Off in Traffic

Traffic. The worst of all contemporary ills. It's where most of us commuters spend hours a day, and it's where the most mild-mannered person can turn into a raving, raging lunatic. But just because we're all susceptible to road rage doesn't make it right to cut people off and drive like a selfish, dangerous prick. There are rules of the road, just like in life. And when someone breaks them, here's what to do.

The WTF Approach to Handling Being F*#!-ing Cut Off

➤ STEP #1: *Give Him the Bird*

People don't flip people off enough. There should be more silent *f*#! yous* on the road, not fewer.

➤ STEP #2: *Cut in Front of Him Repeatedly*

Torture the bastard by cutting in front of him and hitting on the brakes. See how he likes it.

➤ STEP #3: *Hit the Oil Slick Button*

If you're an international spy or you just happen to have the cash, get a real cool James Bond–type of automobile and hit the oil-slick button. Watch the prick spin out of control.

➤ STEP #4: *Follow Him Home and Kill Him*

This only applies to sick f*#!s in creepy places where people often go insane—like California. (There was a famous case in Los Angeles in which a driver, angered that he was honked at, followed the honker home and killed him, his wife, and his two kids. Now *that's* road rage!)

The Great Equalizer

They used to call the gun the "great equalizer" because it enables a small, weak person to kill just as easily as a big, tough one. You just need to be strong enough to pull the trigger.

The automobile is also a great equalizer, which is why you get cut off every day by some snot-nosed teenager driving like an idiot. In their car, everyone feels like a tough guy. If you really are a tough guy, you've got to get out of your car when the traffic stops, smash his window with your elbow, and drag him out onto the street.

54. You're Stuck Behind a Slow Driver on a Windy Mountain Road

Depending on where you live, this situation can be a common occurrence or something that you can't even imagine. "Why would there be a road in a mountain?" an urbanite may ask, in between hocking up a lungful of smog.

Nevertheless, if you ever leave your city, you'll probably find a Sunday driver taking his sweet time driving up an interminably long, windy road, and for some reason that prick won't let you pass.

The WTF Approach to Dealing with a F*#!-ing Sunday Driver

➤ OPTION #1: *Use Your Cell Phone*

Call friends and family members that you wouldn't normally call. Don't tell them the only reason you're calling is because you're bored off your ass.

➤ OPTION #2: *Enjoy the Scenery*

Pull over and take a short walk. Clear your mind, get some exercise, and give the bozo driving 30 MPH a head start. It's been ten years since you've been outside Detroit, so you might as well soak it all in.

➤ OPTION #3: *Go Nuts*

Lean on your horn and start swerving. If he thinks you might follow him to his next stop to kick his ass, he might let you pass.

Road Rules in the Country

Unless you can see the driver, use this guide to determine what type of person is in the vehicle. Be careful who you piss off.

- **RV:** Old retired person. May have army-issued handgun but probably won't use it unless you resemble a Viet Cong.

- **Prius:** Some environmentally conscious yuppie scum taking a drive through the countryside. All they've got to protect themselves are a pair of sculpted legs from yoga class and a lukewarm latte.

- **Black Cadillac:** You may think it's an old person, but it could be a couple of goodfellas. They're probably just as scared of the country as you are, but they've got the guns to kill you and the shovels to hide the evidence.

- **Big dirty truck:** This is what you need to watch out for. These hillbillies have been waiting all week to find a city slicker like you to shoot. And that may be the least of your problems. Think *Deliverance*.

- **Small dirty truck:** You might see one of two kinds of people driving: a day laborer or a hot country girl. You'll know the difference by whether they're blasting mariachi or Shania Twain.

keeping it in the family

55. You Are Asked to Speak at a Funeral

Speaking in public is nerve-racking enough, but speaking at a funeral is the worst. Fact is, you're not a poet—you work in real estate. But that doesn't mean you should decline. Just prepare with a big dose of WTF.

The WTF Approach to F*#!-ing Eulogies

➤ OPTION #1: *Pay Someone*

Put an ad on craigslist for a writer. Give details about the deceased's life, his strengths, his accomplishments, and the nuances of your relationship with him. Give specifics, like the way his scruffy beard felt when he kissed you, how he loved Cuban cigars, or how he used to let you pick which switch on the tree to get beaten with.

➤ OPTION #2: *Rip One Off*

Take a famous eulogy and swap out the details. For instance,

Jawaharlal Nehru had a great one for Gandhi. Keep all the stuff about "divine fire" and "great soul," but cut all the references to India.

➤ OPTION #3: *Fake a Breakdown*

Go up to the podium with several sheets of paper and, after reading a line or two, pause and start crying uncontrollably, occasionally muttering words as if you're trying to speak. Not only is this intensely evocative, but it doesn't require a gift for words.

Option #4: Fill in the Blanks

If you really have nothing to say, use the WTF *Prêt-à-Dire* Eulogy:

_____ was a great (man/woman). (He/She) will always be
[Name]

remembered and will always be in our hearts. In the _____
[number]

years I've known (him/her), (he/she) has always been _____,
[adjective]

_____, and _____. (He/She) was not only my
[adjective]   [adjective]

_____ but also my friend. Every _____, we went to
[relation]   [timeframe]

_____ together, and I will never in my life forget those times.
[place]

I'm sure we all remember the time (he/she) _____. Afterward
[action]

(he/she) told me _____. And I'll never forget those words. In this
[saying or cliché]

world, there are _____ people, and there are _____
[adjective]   [opposite adjective]

people, and I can tell you that _____ was the _____
[Name]   [superlative of adjective]

person I ever met. I will never forget _____, and I will miss (him/
[Name]

her) for the rest of my life. There will never be another _____.
[Name]

SUGGESTED ADJECTIVES

fair, loving, helpful, compassionate, intelligent

56. Your In-Laws Hate You for No Good Reason

Of course they think you're a loser. That's their job. Sure, maybe you're in a band and work at Costco, or maybe you're a writer and you tell dirty jokes in silly little books, but you could also be a brain surgeon. But the facts don't matter—you're just not good enough for Daddy's Little Girl. However, there are ways to win over her parents. Whether it's a dinner at their house or a night out on the town, if you're at your best, you just might be able to make them think you're not a total scumbag.

The WTF Approach to Impressing the F*#!-ing In-Laws

➤ STEP #1: *Know Thy Enemy*

Find out what her father is into and learn enough to listen and ask questions. No need to tell stories or give your opinion unless it's asked for. You get to screw his daughter, so he gets to talk.

➤ STEP #2: *Wear a Tie*

No matter the occasion. You might feel like a schmuck wearing a tie at Applebee's, but that's the point. This shows them that you're willing to look like a schmuck for them.

➤ **STEP #3:** *Come Bearing Gifts*

This is, after all, how you won their daughter over—it wasn't your abs, that's for sure. Get the dad a ship in a bottle. Every older guy likes dumb shit like that.

➤ **STEP #4:** *Pay for Dinner*

Insist that you pay for dinner, even if it's cooked at home.

➤ **STEP #5:** *Do the Dishes*

Nah, *nothing* is worth doing dishes.

for the ladies . . .

"He's not who you think." If you have the kind of parents that don't approve of your husband for who he is, then lie a little. If he's a janitor, confess to them that he really works for the CIA, and is undercover at the local junior high to expose a plot to overthrow the educational system in the United States. Make sure to swear them to secrecy because you can't put him—or them—in danger.

Guess Who's Coming to Dinner

Just like in the movie, parents who don't initially approve of a son-in-law can change their minds. Of course, if her parents don't approve of your relationship based on the color of your skin, you better step up your game and be a pretty damn good match in every other way. It's easier for her bigoted parents to get over their racism when you're acting like Sidney Poitier, and admittedly less so when you're going by "C-note."

Things You Shouldn't Do Around Your Father-In-Law

- Escort your wife by her neck
- Fiddle with his model ships
- Point and laugh at the crucifix on the wall
- Slap your wife's ass
- Slap her mom's ass
- Ask if they swing

57. You Find a Bong in Your Son's Room

Normal, well-adjusted teenage boys share a natural curiosity about three things: sex, drugs, and sports. So if you find a bong in your son's room, don't be too alarmed. Nothing could be more natural (the curiosity—not the weed).

That said, while beer is the *real* gateway drug, pot is illegal, and smoking too much of it will slow him down and result in poor clothing choices. Also, you don't want him to move on to more serious addictions that are a direct result of marijuana such as eating cookies, listening to Pink Floyd, and taking a hacky sack wherever he goes.

The WTF Approach to Stopping Your Kid from Smoking F*#!-ing Weed

▶ **OPTION #1: *Tell Him Where Drugs Come From***

If your son gives you that "it's natural" and "God gave him the plant" crap, tell him that he's an idiot. Almost every drug comes from a natural source—heroine from poppies and cocaine from coco leaves. On second thought, if you tell him this, it might not

scare him, but make him curious about growing other drugs. And before you know it he'll have green thumbs—not just green bud.

➤ OPTION #2: *Pretend to Call a Cop*

If you really want to nip his weed addiction in the "bud," wait until he is really high and then have a friend come over dressed as a cop. Let him in, and have him tell your kid that, using his new thought-reading machine, he knows he's high on pot. Let him add that he has a hidden camera following your son to watch his every move. This will scare the shit out of your boy. By the time he figures out it's a joke, he'll be so petrified that drugs will be the last thing on his mind.

➤ OPTION #3: *Join Him*

Sometimes kids do things to rebel against their parents. If you join your son and smoke with him, he'll be so annoyed he'll quit toking the reefer before he can say, "marijuana." If there's any hesitation, make sure to invite all his friends over and hang out with them.

HOW YOUR KID SPENDS HIS WEEKEND		
Activity	*Before Pot*	*After Pot*
Sleeping	30%	30%
Eating	5%	30%
Jerking off	65%	30%
Researching New Weed	0%	10%

With or without pot, you're kid's a moron. At least with it, he wastes his time more evenly.

58. You Find Out That You're Adopted

Imagining that the parents who raised you are not your real parents after all might put a smile on your face, but what if it were really true? What would you do if you found out that you were actually adopted? For those of you in this predicament, consider these rules before you start searching for your real mommy and daddy—you know, the ones who didn't want you in the first place.

The WTF Approach to Dealing with Being F*#!-ing Adopted

➤ STEP #1: *Get Therapy*

Everyone who finds out they're adopted has issues—namely abandonment issues. A therapist can help you work through this by talking about your emotional problems. Don't worry about the cost; your adoptive parents who love and adore you will feel guilty and foot the bill.

➤ STEP #2: *Don't Look for Your Birth Parents*

They gave you up for a reason. They *hated* you.

Or . . .

➤ STEP #2: *Track Down Your Birth Parents*

. . . But only if you plan to systematically destroy their lives, cripple them with guilt, and wind up with a fat check in your hand for all your emotional pain and suffering.

➤ STEP #3: *Love Your Adoptive Parents*

Put the past behind you and be happy with the parents you have. They raised you, so don't be an ungrateful little bastard. Of course, technically, you *are* a bastard.

YOU'RE NOT MY DADDY

Too many adopted kids think they can stay out late and do whatever they want after they find out that their adopted parents aren't their birth parents. Just because you didn't come from your dad's sperm and your mother's egg doesn't mean that they are not your parents. They are. But that doesn't mean you have to listen to them. No one listens to their parents.

WHAT THE F*#! IS UP WITH . . . "KID-CRAZY" CELEBRITIES

Some people make fun of Angelina Jolie because she adopts a lot of kids, as if she were "kid crazy" or something. But what she does is great. Imagine these kids living in a Third World country rather than having a wholesome childhood in Hollywood with a superstar mom who traverses the globe looking for another child to cheer her up. What could be a better, more normal childhood than that?

How to Tell If You're Adopted

If you suspect you are adopted but aren't sure, here are warning signs:

- ❏ You're black and your parents are from Wales.

- ❏ Your dad has a substantially bigger penis than you.

- ❏ You have no baby pictures.

- ❏ You have two mommies.

- ❏ You are ugly and your parents are hot.

59. You Find Out You're Cut Out of Your Parents' Will

It's happened to many an heir apparent, Tori Spelling and Baron Hilton famously among them. Your parents decide to cut you out of their will or to leave you a tiny percentage of their wealth. Those animals! You've put up with their nagging, their boring stories, and their pitiful expressions of love for years, and for what? To be left out in the cold, just as you saw the bright, shimmering light at the end of the tunnel—at the same time they did, no less.

The WTF Approach to Getting Your F"#!-ing Slice of the Pie

➤ OPTION #1: *Pull an Anna Nicole*

Take your parent's estate to court. Be sure to fabricate proof of you and your parent's loving relationship. For example, crayon drawings of you and mommy, soaked in tea to authenticate their age.

➤ OPTION #2: *Pay Off a Nurse*

Have a nurse testify that your deceased parents requested that the will be changed on their death bed to leave you everything.

➤ OPTION #3: *Discredit Your Siblings*

Start gathering evidence to make the case that you deserve your siblings' shares. Point to the You-Tube video of your sister in New Orleans on Mardi Gras working it for beads.

➤ OPTION #4: *Guard Fluffy*

In the instance that your parents have left everything to a pet, be sure to establish yourself as the most appropriate guardian for the mutt. Then, promptly help the mongrel write a will, complete with pawprint. Afterward, run over Fluffy in your new Bentley.

➤ OPTION #5: *Blackmail the Poor*

When the poor impoverish you, get back your money. If your self-ish parents gave everything to charity, blackmail is your best option. Assure the charity that you will keep them in court for the next decade unless they pay you handsomely to be their spokesperson.

When All Else Fails . . .

So none of the above worked in your favor and now you're on the verge of being broke—take one of these last-ditch efforts:

- If your parents were in the public eye, write a book outing your father as a homosexual or sell the movie rights to your life story, complete with child abuse charges (no one's left to refute them!).

- Start a business helping other would-be heirs protect their future assets.

- Blow the rest of your money on coke and whores. If you're going to be broke anyway, you might as well go out in style.

- Get a job. Work. Just friggin' work, you spoiled brat!

60. Your Preteen Kids Ask You about Sex

You've been dreading this conversation since you saw the sonogram. And now the little brats beat you to it. Instead of waiting for you to have a well-thought-out speech prepared, they start asking you questions. Your kiddies keep hearing about penises and vaginas in school and they start asking you questions like: "Where do babies come from?" "Why does mommy scream at night?" and "What brand of lubrication is best for anal?" How to deal? Try this:

The WTF Approach to F*#!-ing Impromptu Sex-Ed

➤ OPTION #1: *Lie*

If you think you can get away with it, lie to your kids and stick to stories about storks and other nonsense. After all, you've already lied to them about Santa Claus, so why stop now?

➤ OPTION #2: *Use Clever Metaphors*

Saying daddy drives his choo-choo train into mommy's love tunnel might sound better than saying that daddy shoves his fat cock into mommy's little pussy.

▶ OPTION #3: *Make Sex Sound Icky*

The other way to go about explaining sex—particularly if your kids are too old and too savvy for the "choo-choo" routine—is to explain in medical detail what actually happens during intercourse. It would turn anyone off.

▶ OPTION #4: *Let Them Watch You Have Sex*

If watching you and the old lady go at it all night like depraved animals won't answer their questions once and for all about sex and turn them off from it, nothing will.

NOTE: WTF is not responsible for the thousands of dollars in therapy it's going to take to correct your kids after letting them watch you and your wife. That's your own damn fault.

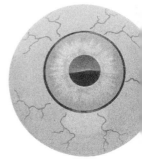

REMEMBERING RODNEY

"What a kid I got, I told him about the birds and the bees and he told me about the butcher and my wife."

—Rodney Dangerfield

61. You Find Out Your Teenage Daughter Is Having Sex

Unprotected teenage sex is not the problem it used to be in the United States. Safe sex and abstinence programs have significantly decreased the number of adolescent mishaps. But that doesn't do you much good if you find out that your daughter is one of those girls getting an early start. Here's what to do if you want to avoid being a very, very pissed off grandparent:

The WTF Approach to Handling Your F*#!-ing Sexually Active Daughter

➤ STEP #1: *Blame Each Other*

When your child does anything wrong or unwise, it is best to vent your frustration by blaming your spouse or ex-spouse for teaching her bad habits and being a bad influence. This is much easier than facing up to the problem at hand and dealing with it like the adults that you claim to be.

➤ STEP #2: *Beat the Living Shit Out of Her Boyfriend*

It won't help the situation any and your daughter will hate you for it, but it might make you feel better.

➤ STEP #3: *Disown Her*

She has tainted herself and the family's good name. God be with her. She is going to need all the help she can get. Just not from you.

Teenagers Like Sex

Kids get bored and have intercourse. It's always been that way and it always will be. So don't beat yourself up about it happening. The only way to stop your daughter from having sex is to instill in her the fear that she will burn for eternity in hell if she does so. Even then, this threat will only work until she's sick of giving blowjobs.

YOUR DAUGHTER MIGHT BE HAVING SEX IF . . .

- She dyes her hair different colors

- She wears makeup

- She likes pop music

- She likes to dance

- She's always on the phone

- She wants a car

- She likes reality TV

- You're not as close as you used to be

- She's a slut and you *know* it.

62. You Realize You're Going Bald . . . at Twenty-Five

Like your father and his father before him, you knew this day would come—only a few pathetic strands remain from your once thick, glorious mane. But before your thirtieth birthday? *Really*? Though you've tried Rogaine, Propecia, and similar products, utter baldness is inevitable. Try the following alternatives instead.

The WTF Approach to Tackling F*#!-ing Baldness

➤ **OPTION #1:** *The Comb-Over*

Sweep your hair from the good side all the way across your bald head. This is a fantastic, timeless hair style and absolutely conceals any male pattern baldness without arousing any suspicion. Use an entire bottle of hairspray and pray for no wind.

➤ **OPTION #2:** *Use Spray-on-Hair*

This only works with dark hair, and even then not well. Avoid rain.

➤ **OPTION #3:** *Wear More Hats*

You can pay homage to some of your favorite heroes, such as Davy Crocket, Abe Lincoln, or Otto von Bismarck. Or you can become a cowboy, a nineteenth-century gentleman, a 1930s businessman, or even wear a turban and say you're

a sultan. However, if you decide to rock the turban, you should probably wear a baseball cap when you fly.

➤ OPTION #4: *Convert to Judaism*

If you choose to become an Orthodox Jew, you'll have to cover your head at all times in public due to a strict dress code. While the religion's strict rules will successfully hide your hair loss, the downside is that you'll need to be circumcised. If you already are, you might even have to have more taken off.

NOTE: The rare double circumcision is only practiced by extremist and abnormally well-hung Jewish sects—think Ron Jeremy dressed as a rabbi . . . without pants.

➤ OPTION #5: *Become Amish*

In addition to the hat, Amish women don't judge men by the thickness of their hair, but on how fast they can raise a barn.

➤ OPTION #6: *Bic Your Head and Work Out*

If you're African American, going bald is no big deal. There are countless bald black sex symbols—and you've got that "well endowed" thing going for you anyway.

It's a little tougher for white guys to pull it off, but it's not impossible. Notable bald, sexy white men include Bruce Willis, Mr. Clean, and the guy from *Kojak*.

➤ OPTION #7: *Get New Friends*

If you hang out with only fat guys, even if you're bald, you'll look better. Unless, of course, you're both fat and bald.

➤ OPTION #8: *Ride a Bike Everywhere*

This will do two things. It will get you in shape and improve your overall appearance, and it will give you a reason to never take off your helmet. This is a great way to hide your growing bald spot, as long as your bike is nearby.

for the ladies . . .

All isn't lost if you're starting to lose your hair. Sinead O'Connor, Britney Spears, and Sigourney Weaver in *Alien III* all made being bald sexy. Nevertheless, you better be able to make up for it in the bedroom.

➤ OPTION #9: *Get Wacky*

Glue feathers to your head and tell anyone who asks that you're undergoing a metamorphosis that will eventually turn you into a turkey. After all, becoming a giant bird is better than being just another bald guy.

WTFACT: The Vikings tried an odd hair loss remedy—rubbing goose crap all over the scalp. It didn't work. Why do you think they wore such ridiculous hats?

63. You Find Your Thirteen-Year-Old Sister's Ass on MySpace

The Internet is dangerous. Not only does it allow children easy access to porn, but with a few clicks, your little baby sis might just broadcast her own. Soon pedophiles from all over the world are messaging her about how "bootylicious" she is, how they enjoy the "junk in her trunk," and how much they'd like to "tap dat ass."

The WTF Approach to Stopping a F*#!-ing e-Lolita

➤ **STEP #1: *Don't Believe Her***

Refuse to accept anything she says as the truth. Not a single word. Only one in 100,000 teenage girls ever speaks the truth.

➤ **STEP #2: *Limit Her Private Time***

Put her computer in the living room so you can see whether she's writing a report on cross-cultural communication or browsing interracial porn.

➤ **STEP #3: *Refuse to Allow Her to Have a Webcam***

Keeping a webcam off the computer not only reduces the chances that your kid sister's ass will show up on MySpace or

a video of her dancing around will make it onto YouTube, it also reduces the chance she'll wind up on PornSpace or YouPorn—at least anytime soon.

Attention: They Aren't Real Friends

Hate to break it to you MySpace morons, but you really don't have 30,000 friends, no matter what you think. Don't believe it? Try posting in your next blog that you need help moving, then see how many responses you get.

WHAT THE F*#! IS UP WITH . . . cRaZy!!! PHOTOS

Why is it that every chick on MySpace has the same photos? You know, the ones of her and "the girls" out on the town. The night where all they did was take friggin' pictures! Ladies, make sure that you don't forget to post the one where you're licking a bottle which you aptly titled "cRaZy!!!" For the record, you should just call it "stupid."

in the **bedroom**

WTF?!

64. You Wake Up Next to a "10 at 2:00, 2 at 10:00"

If you wake up after a night of drinking and debauchery next to a surprisingly ugly bedmate, you've already broken the cardinal rule of drunk sex: *Never* spend the night with someone you brought home while in a drunken stupor. If it's your place, kick her out. If it's her place, catch a cab. Either way, the minute you've climaxed, get free of this person immediately. Because no matter how sober you think you are, there's a good chance that what seemed like a "10 at 2 A.M." will end up being a "2 at 10 A.M."

For those of you who need the cuddling as much as the sex, here's what to do if you find yourself entangled with a monster after what seemed like a fabulous night.

If you're at her place . . .

➤ OPTION #1: *Leave Quietly*

If you wake up in a stranger's bed and the animal is still sound asleep, get your shit and get the hell out as fast as you can. If you feel guilty about this, leave an apple by her pillow as a token of your appreciation and respect.

If she's really, really ugly, feel free to poison the apple for revenge.

➤ OPTION #2: *Stay with Her*

If you stay with the same person long enough, chances are, there will come a point when you're going to have to be drunk to have sex with her anyway. Stick it out and get to know each other.

➤ OPTION #3: *The Quick Excuse and Run*

Here are some good excuses to shout over your shoulder as you leave the beast's lair:

- Late for work (yes, doctors work on Sunday)
- Family member in the hospital
- Late for church
- Reservations at exclusive brunch (wish you could come, but they're totally booked)
- Cable guy's coming

If She's at Your Place . . .

➤ OPTION #1: *Emergency!*

"Oh my god! I'm so sorry. Wake up, please! Sorry, gorgeous, but you're going to have to leave. I hate to do this (*wink, wink*) but my mother just called and she's in town for a surprise visit. I'm sorry, but you have to leave."

> **OPTION #2. Say You're Married**

If you *are* married, you're a schmuck and you get what you deserve. If you're not, tell the "2" you are. After you get lectured, she'll be on her way. If the "2" chooses to stay, then, even though she's ugly, you have to admit it's kind of hot that she doesn't care about things like that.

> **OPTION #3: Play Dead**

If you're a real coward, play dead. Don't move and barely breathe. When she goes to call 911, make a run for it. You could get lucky. If she's a real romantic, she might kill herself like in *Romeo and Juliet*, leaving you off the hook for good.

IN THE FUTURE . . .

Stop drinking so much. Learn your lesson, and don't hit the bottle so hard. Make yet another pledge to only bang chicks you've seen before you put on your beer goggles.

65. You Realize That You Are Gay

The consensus now is that if you're gay, you were born that way. Nothing you can do about it. Sure, you can join the priesthood and try to suppress it (we've seen how successful that plan is), but chances are, you'll eventually be living life as a homosexual no matter how much you fight it. It's what you were destined to do.

The WTF Approach to Coming Out of the F*#!-ing Closet

➤ STEP #1: *Cancel Your Fishing Trip*

Unless you're fishing for cock or hunting for dick, you're no longer obligated to fish or hunt.

➤ STEP #2: *Get a Decent Haircut*

Now that you're officially gay, you're not going to be able to go to Super Cuts for your next 'do.

You're probably going to have to get a new wardrobe, and throw out the wagon-wheel coffee table as well. You don't want to be an embarrassment to your new community.

➤ STEP #3: *Come Out in Style*

There's no reason why coming out of the closet and announcing

your gay lifestyle has to be a grim, serious affair. Try to make it fun. Take your dad to a baseball game and have it announced on the scoreboard in front of thousands of fans and millions watching at home. He'd appreciate the effort.

➤ STEP #4: *Spill the Beans, Save the Franks*

Coming out of the closet isn't easy. It's got to be one of the hardest things to do. (Not that we would know. We don't want readers to get the wrong idea. We're not gay. Not that there's anything wrong with it. To each his own, you know. We're just not gay, so please don't get that idea just because we're writing about it. Not that there's anything wrong with that!)

WTFACT: Approximately one in every ten people is homosexual. You are not alone!

Gay Family Values

An argument propagated by conservatives against the legalization of gay marriage is that it would corrode the institution and lead to a further decay of "family values." Really? Well, here is some information for you bozos: Massachusetts was the first state to allow gay marriage and it also consistently ranks among the top states for the lowest divorce rate. It's true, and the Bible Belt states—whose political leaders constantly taunt "family values"—have the highest divorce rates.

YOU MIGHT BE A HOMOSEXUAL IF . . .

❏ You went to boarding school in England.

❏ You cook a lot and you're not Italian or French.

❏ You're white and you can dance.

❏ You have a flair for fashion.

❏ You want to have sex with men . . . *a lot.*

66. You're about to Have Sex and Find Out You're Out of Condoms

Unless you're a virgin, in which case you're probably not reading this book (you know the phrase, "old enough to read, old enough to . . ."), you've been in a situation where you're about to get your groove on only to find out that you're fresh out of condoms.

Being hard up for a rubber in the heat of the moment is quite possibly one of the worst things you can experience (though not getting an opportunity to use a condom is worse). Nevertheless, if you're about to ride bareback on a new pony, you better think twice: It might just save your life.

The WTF Approach to Not Having Any F*#!-ing Condoms

➤ **STEP #1:** *Just Say No!*

If it helps, think of Nancy Regan saying it—spread eagle wearing nothing—nothing but wrinkles, that is.

➤ **STEP #2:** *Remember: There Is No Substitute*

Saran Wrap, plastic baggies, and aluminum foil don't work. Trust us. It's not worth even trying.

➤ STEP #2.5: *When It's Worth Trying*

If she's really, *really* hot and doesn't *look* like she has an STD—double-bag it and secure it with a rubberband or a twisty-tie.

> **NOTE:** If you're desperate enough to try this out, WTF applauds your creativity but will not pay for any hospital bills. We will, however, suggest ironic baby names like Ziploc, Glad, and Hefty.

➤ STEP #3: *Know What Not to Do*

- Use that old lambskin condom. Stay away from lambskin condoms! First of all, they don't stop diseases, and second of all, they're made from baby sheep intestines and smell like a farm, which shouldn't be sexy—except to a sheep. Hmm . . .

- Opt for the pull-out method. If venereal disease isn't scary enough for you, consider having a baby with that barfly you took home. Yikes.

- Let *her* bang *you*.

Location, Location, Location

If you're in Africa, Asia, or certain parts of Florida, you might find that the locals don't even know what condoms are, let alone endorse their use. Some tribal cultures even believe that using a condom is a sin because it separates a man from his partner.

Good luck trying that one with the chick from *Match.com*.

IN THE FUTURE . . .

Live by the Boy Scout motto: Always be prepared. Jogging half a mile to the store with a hard on is not an option. (Though every Boy Scout has played that game . . . right?) And, depending on your particular proclivities, you may want to keep several sizes on hand.

67. Your New Girlfriend Giggles at Your Penis

You knew you weren't big. You never thought you'd be a porn star. But laughable? WTF?

The WTF Approach to Working with What You're F*#!-ing Packing

➤ OPTION #1: *Learn Cunnilingus*

If you think this is a foreign language, your sex knowledge obviously needs some work. Either rent some girl-on-girl porn and practice on the back of your hand, or find an older woman. She'll turn you into a pro.

➤ OPTION #2: *Date a Dwarf Instead*

If you aren't big enough for her, try an Asian dwarf.

➤ OPTION #3: *Shave Your Pubic Hair*

This will make your penis at least appear bigger. You can also try applying some light foundation down the middle of your shaft, making your penis appear longer. However, it will also make your penis look thinner. So, if girth is your problem, use horizontally striped condoms and practice gyrating in giant circles.

> **OPTION #4: *Get a Big Truck***

This always compensates for a small penis. After all, how could a guy with such a big truck and such big wheels have a small dick?

> **OPTION #5: *Make More Money***

Nobody's perfect. Since you've got no bulge in the front of your pants, make sure that in the back there's a fat wallet stuffed with $100 bills. Many women will find you irresistible. There are a lot more gold-diggers than size queens out there anyway.

> **OPTION #6: *Get a Dildo***

Nowadays, sex toys are far better than a real penis. The only thing they don't do yet is cuddle her. So practice your spooning because that's all you're good for.

> **OPTION #7: *Five Rubbers***

You might not feel shit, but at least she will.

> **OPTION #8: *Become a Priest***

If you live up to your vows, you won't use it anyway.

68. Your Girlfriend Starts Getting Too Kinky in Bed

Most guys complain that their girlfriends aren't kinky enough. "You want to put what *where*?" she flinches. "You want to do *what* with another girl?" she asks—though this time, she can't help but be a little curious. But what if you're one of the few guys whose girlfriend isn't just kinky, but *too* kinky?

Crazy, kinky sex can be a slippery slope. At first it was enough to cover each other with whipped cream. Then, before you know it, twin midget transsexuals are living in your closet. Be careful—before you know it, she'll be turning the kink up to eleven. Follow our approach if you don't want things to get out of hand.

The WTF Approach to Curbing the F*#!-ing Kink

> **OPTION #1: *Have Less Sex***

The only way to make normal, "vanilla" sex exciting—or even worth doing—is to do it less often. Go on a trip, get sick, or just tell her that you have a headache. This will make her want sex more and appreciate *any* kind—even the boring kind that you're capable of giving. However, there's a risk with this strategy. She might feel that you are less interested in her, and therefore spend more time trying to seduce you in extra kinky ways, such as lying on the coffee table spread eagle when you get home—with a bald eagle on her lap.

> **OPTION #2: *Give Her to the Gardener***

If you really can't satisfy her appetite for wacky sex, find someone who can. Make the gardener or the pool boy or your driver screw her silly. You might as well pay people to handle *all* your chores.

> **OPTION #3: *Develop a Disgusting Fetish***

One way to bring her kink down to a manageable level is to become too kinky yourself, thus scaring her into regular sex. If you are unseemly hairy or fat, wearing a simple lace teddy will turn down her kink in a heartbeat.

REMEMBERING RODNEY

" I'm a bad lover. I once caught a peeping tom booing me. "

—Rodney Dangerfield

Here are some other kinky fetishes that are sure to turn her off:

- Ask her for a blumpkin—if you don't know what this is . . . google it!

- Wear diapers and a bib like a fat baby, suck on your thumb, and make her change you.

- Shave your pubic hair, roll it into a ball, and eat it like a cat.

➤ **OPTION #4:** *Talk to Her*

It's the last thing you want to do and it's one hell of a chore. But sometimes, if you speak really slow and look her in the eye, you can actually communicate with her. She might even listen— though it's doubtful.

KINK SCALE

1. Missionary position only

2. Doggy style, oral, and the occasional 69

3. Light spanking and hair pulling

4. Anal, rim jobs, and facials

5. Dildos, butt plugs, and sex with a porno on the flat screen

6. Threesomes, sex in public, and fisting

7. Heavy bondage

8. Cunnilingus during menstruation after a jog on a hot summer day

9. Fecalfelia, golden showers, and bestiality

10. Necrophilia

11. Necro-bestiality in public on a hot summer day—or fucking a dead donkey in the middle of the mall

69. Your Girlfriend Gives You Herpes

The news is in. Those itchy little bumps on your penis aren't a temporary rash you got from eating shellfish. You've got herpes, dipshit, and all signs point to your girlfriend. Before you start screaming at her, follow these rules.

The WTF Approach to Dealing with Your F*#!-ing STD-Giving Girlfriend

> **STEP #1:** *Resent Her*

Say that you understand and forgive her, but secretly resent her for the rest of your life. You know you're going to anyway.

> **STEP #2:** *Guilt Her When Appropriate*

Whenever you want something to go your way, just remind her of the scorching sores on your penis. That should make her feel guilty enough to give in.

> **STEP #3:** *Determine If She Knew She Had Them*

Check her medicine cabinet. If there are no clues, call her doctor and ask to renew a prescription for herpes medication. If you can, use a female friend to make the call. As a last resort, break into her gynecologist's office to find her files. If you get caught, tell them that your herpes outbreak drove you temporarily insane.

➤ **STEP #4: *Get Retested***

Herpes might be the least of your problems. Get tested . . . for *everything*.

➤ **STEP #5: *Leave Her and Join* PositiveSingles.com**

This is an extensive website for hip young singles covered in sores. (Yes, this is a real website.)

WTFACT: About one in five Americans have herpes, but 80 percent of these people are unaware of it. Pull down your pants and check . . . *now*!

➤ **STEP #6: *Audition for a Herpes Medication Commercial***

You'll be able to claim that you're not just a paid actor, but an actual user of the product. This may offer you the break you need to take over the entertainment industry.

WTF ABOUT TOWN

We recently interviewed a particularly vocal herpe about his hopes, dreams, and plans for the future.

WTF: Can you please state your name for the record?

Herpe: Herpes Simplex 2.

WTF: What's the difference between you and those Simplex 1 characters?

Herpe: They're an embarrassment. They hang out on the mouth, usually on the outside, and can even be mistaken for a pimple. Those ain't herpes, they're cold sores. They're afraid to go down and do the dirty work where the sun don't shine.

WTF: What do you say to people with herpes who complain about the itchiness and pain you guys cause?

Herpe: Life's tough. You think that I chose this lifestyle? Do you think if I could choose my destiny, this would be it?

WTF: If you could pop up anywhere, where would you choose?

Herpe: I'd choose Angelina Jolie's lips . . . either pair.

70. Your Lover Answers the Phone During Sex

You're so close, and you think she is too (not that you ever know for sure if she can—with you). Then the phone rings. Once, twice, and, before the third ring she's off of you and chatting away. WTF?

Nothing is more annoying than being interrupted during the heights of passion—at least for *you*. What do you do when your lover answers the phone during sex in order to make sure it doesn't happen again?

The WTF Approach to F*#!-ing Intercourse Hangups

> **OPTION #1: *Determine the Importance of the Call***

If your lover's a doctor, you're going to have to deal. Your orgasm may be important, but the life of a five-year-old kid hovering between life and death takes precedence . . . unless it's been a really, really long time.

So it better be a matter of life or death if she can't wait the two minutes it takes to have sex in order to call back.

> **OPTION #2: *Count to Sixty Then Finish Yourself Off***

There's no reason to wait for your lover to get off. Teach your lover a

lesson and do it yourself. After all, there's no touch more skilled than your own.

➤ OPTION #3: *Make a Phone Call*

Two can play at that game. Stay on the phone long after she hangs up. When your lover tries to get back to business, tell her to wait. You're on the phone, for Christ's sake.

➤ OPTION #4: *Turn It into a Sex Game*

Just because she has to answer the phone doesn't mean the sex has to stop. Continue pleasuring her while she tries to maintain a conversation. If you want to get really kinky, don't hold back and let the person on the line join the fun. If they're down with it, maybe he'll start talking dirty. Who knows? This could turn into a regular thing. But tread carefully. If it gets too whacky, the next time you call her, she could be at his place.

IN THE FUTURE . . .

Secretly put the phone on silent before you start. This way, there will be no calls and you can continue uninterrupted. When she goes to the bathroom, turn her ringer back on. With luck, the phone will ring so you can relax.

71. Your Mom Catches You Masturbating

If you have ever been caught spanking your monkey by your mom, you understand what true horror is: the image of your mother's mortified face forever etched in your memory. If you find yourself in this sticky situation, here's what to do.

The WTF Approach to Being F*#!-ing Caught by Your Mom

➤ OPTION #1: *Wash Up and Apologize*

This particular option is best if your mom happens to be very conservative or religious. Apologize to her and promise that you will never do it again. Tell her that Satan took hold of your hand and, through the power of his evil genius, forced you to do it.

➤ OPTION #2: *Flip the Switch*

Try turning it around on her. Blame her for her lack of respect for your privacy. She should have knocked. You can also scold her for not letting you bring home a girl to have sex with, thus forcing you to masturbate. Reinforce that she has no right to tell you what to do with your body, and that masturbation is normal, healthy, and a good way to pass the time.

➤ OPTION #3: *Pretend Nothing Happened*

If you just pretend nothing happened and never bring it up,

your mom will do the same. She probably wants the image of you stroking yourself out of her head—desperately.

➤ OPTION #4: *Quit Masturbating*

Yeah . . . right.

The WTF Approach to What Not to Do

Do not ask for help: Even if the particular bathroom where you're jerking off happens to be in the Deep South, asking your mom to help you climax is *not* okay—even if you just want her to watch and cheer you on. Now, a stepsister— that's a different story altogether.

Do not continue: No matter how close you are to finishing, the minute your mom sees your erect penis pointed toward the sky, you should discontinue your masturbatory session immediately, as a show of decency and respect to the woman who gave you life. Once she splits, game on.

Do not deny it: No matter how gullible your mother is, there is no way you can convince her that you had an itch. She gets itches too, and when she does, she scratches them, she doesn't yank them.

Do not feel ashamed: If your mother tries to make you feel guilty, don't let her. Who brought you into this world, a stork?

Do You Masturbate Too Much?

Yes, it is possible. If you answer yes to one of these questions, you might have a problem:

❑ When you cum, does smoke come out?

❑ Is there a palmprint on your penis?

❑ Are the ends of your pubes singed?

❑ Instead of a cum-rag, do you use a Q-tip?

❑ Are your balls flat?

72. The Ladies Call You the "One-Minute Man"

What are you, thirteen? This has to stop. If you can't keep it going long enough for a lady to be interested in another test drive, it's time to learn what's up.

The WTF Approach to Avoiding an Early F*#!-ing Release

➤ OPTION #1: *Take Meds*

You'd be surprised what kind of medications are available nowadays. They have pills not only to get your dick up, but also to stop it from going down too quickly. But beware of the side effects, especially with some of those ancient Chinese herbs.

➤ OPTION #2: *Wear a Condom*

This is a pretty good advice any way. It can save a life, stop you from being a parent, and significantly decrease your sexual pleasure. Using a condom will work if your problem is that you have an extra-sensitive pee pee, but not if the problem is all in your head.

➤ OPTION #3: *Don't Go Out with a Loaded Gun*

If lasting more than a minute requires that you jerk it thirty times beforehand, do it.

➤ OPTION #4: *Think about Baseball*

If you think about something that doesn't turn you on, this will take your mind off your problem. If the sport itself isn't enough, picture the baseball team naked. This will work, unless you get turned on by sweaty guys in tight pants swinging large bats. In this case, think of women's volleyball players instead. A sport people of all sexual orientations can think of is women's basketball.

➤ OPTION #5: *Get an Uglier Girlfriend*

Maybe she's just too hot for you and your penis, so try downgrading. If you're not sure you want to ditch your lady before you test out your theory, hang out at WNBA games and chat up the girls. Don't worry about breaking her heart—at this rate, she'll be walking out on you soon anyway.

73. After a Night of Drinking You Wet the Bed

Many kids wet the bed at night, turning their clean bedsheets into a pool of piss. It's relatively normal. But as an adult, you're up shit (or rather piss) creek.

Wetting the bed after a night of drinking can cost adults relationships, friends, and ton of laundry soap. The obvious thing to do is to stop drinking and see if you can now go to bed piss free. But we at WTF would never encourage you to be a teetotaler, so here are steps you can take:

The WTF Approach to Avoiding a Wet F*#!-ing Bed

➤ OPTION #1: *Wear Diapers*

The obvious thing to do is to wear diapers when you sleep. After all, you're a big friggin' baby anyway, so you might as well act like one.

➤ OPTION #2: *Sleep in the Bathtub*

Invest in a Jacuzzi and enjoy a good, clean night's sleep.

➤ OPTION #3: *Get a Giant Litter Box*

You can build one yourself, or you can try to purchase one from a lion tamer.

WTFACT: Approximately 1 in 100 adults wet the bed—drink or no drink. Eww.

➤ OPTION #4: *Dream of the Desert*

Listening to waterfalls and streams flowing is a common tool to help lull many an insomniac to sleep, but it's the last thing you want to do. You could look for a tape of sounds of the desert instead. Common sounds of the desert are rattlesnakes, sandstorm winds, and, in some regions, violent Anti-American rhetoric.

Date Someone Who Can Help

You might be able to find assistance and support from a special someone:

- **Date a nurse.** Try shacking up with her. She might find your repulsive habit cute and child-like. Plus, she's used to people pissing themselves like animals anyway.

- **Date a laundress.** Finally, someone who doesn't mind washing sheets over and over again.

- **Date a pervert.** There are a surprising number of people out there with a urine fetish of some sort. Date one of these perverts and she'll enjoy the surprise wet spot.

dealing with the mrs.

74. You Suspect Your Partner Is Cheating

Something's not right. She's changed. There's a bounce in her step and you didn't put it there. Not only that, but she's out of town five days a week.

The WTF Approach to Catching a Possible F*#!-ing Adulterer

➤ STEP #1: *Do Some Investigating Yourself*

Check her phone. Check her car. Look for unfamiliar hairs on her jacket, blouse, and panties.

➤ STEP #2: *Hire a Sleuth*

Make sure to get her on tape. In most states, this will be the difference between her getting everything you've worked so hard for, and her only getting half.

➤ STEP #3: *Get Creative*

Anonymously send her flowers and see if she tells you about them.

REMEMBERING RODNEY

"I have good-looking kids. Thank goodness my wife cheats on me."

—Rodney Dangerfield

➤ STEP #4: *Flip the Switch*

Start having an affair. If she begins to suspect you of having an affair, chances are she's not having one. Otherwise, wrapped up in her own infidelity, she's unlikely to notice. She'll be too busy trying to cover for herself. Of course, this could also mean that you're cheating when she's not, but you just *have* to find out.

➤ STEP #5: *Get Even*

If your detective work proves she's a cheating whore, send any incriminating e-mails that you find to everyone from her ninety-five-year-old grandmother to the mailman to Anderson Cooper.

REASONS TO EXPECT YOUR PARTNER IS CHEATING

- She left the house smelling like Chanel No. 5, and came home smelling like cum.

- Her hair looks like she's been driving around in a convertible all day, but she drives an SUV.

- Every time she has to "work late," she comes home and showers immediately.

- You find a box of extra-large condoms in her bag, and, well, those aren't yours.

- She keeps getting "wrong number" calls.

- When she does want to have sex with you, it's a lot kinkier.

- . . . Or conversely, she looks even more bored.

75. You Discover the Girl You're Dating Is a Dude

You've kissed her, you've felt her up, but you and your new sexy lady have yet to go all the way. There's a reason for this and it's not that she's waiting for the "right" time like she says. But you can't wait any longer. So you try and spice things up by jumping into the shower with her. You open the curtains and . . . bam! Your chick's got a dick. Now what?

The WTF Approach to Dating a F*#!-ing Tranny

➤ OPTION #1: *Call* Jerry Springer

Finally you can be a guest on your favorite show. Call *The Jerry Springer Show* and tell them your story. If you get picked as a guest, you can share your folly with the whole world, including your parents and close friends. Make sure to act surprised when your "girlfriend" confesses that she's a dude. Then, as is customary on the show, hit her until the bodyguards drag you off.

➤ OPTION #2: *Make Her Go All the Way*

For decades, science has been able to successfully transform a penis into a fully functional vagina.

In fact, using the most sensitive parts of the penis, doctors can create a clitoris that's just as good—if not better—than the genuine article. Studies suggest that these new girls on the block have less trouble having an orgasm than their natural sisters.

➤ OPTION #3: *Find a Real Chick*

Finding a chick without a dick that is just as bitchy and annoying shouldn't be difficult.

➤ OPTION #4: *Ignore It*

You like the girl. She's smart, she's sexy, she's sweet. So, she has a dick. Nobody's perfect.

WTF: UP CLOSE AND PERSONAL

For those of you macho men that are confident that you would never mistake a guy for a girl, I can assure you that anything is possible. I once felt the same way. Until, on a mild spring day in Manhattan, I was proven wrong.

During the annual Puerto Rican Day parade in 1999, I came across one of the most beautiful women I had ever seen. She was exotic, elegant, and had the kind of body that made me drop to my knees and thank God I'm a man. Unfortunately, after a romantic afternoon of flirting, kissing, and some mild touching, she confessed to me that so was she! But beggars can't be choosers . . .

—GB

76. You Can't Get Control of the Remote Control

After sex, kids, and money, control over the television is one of the most heavily disputed subjects in every household. You want to watch the ballgame, and she wants to watch some *Lifetime* movie about a teenage mother with breast cancer.

The WTF Approach to the F*#!-ing Remote Battle

➤ **STEP #1:** *Give Middle-of-the-Road Channels a Shot*

Don't go for the black and white of ESPN versus Lifetime. Instead try out the History Channel, Home & Garden TV, and VH1. You'll be surprised how much you might like shows about fixing up houses to sell them for more money, or how riveting news about Britney Spears's latest spectacle can be. The same goes for you, ladies. Before you know it, thirteenth-century European battle formations will be your favorite topic—after Britney Spears, of course.

➤ **STEP #2:** *Get Another Television*

Prerequisites for any successful marriage are two TVs, two cars, and two bank accounts (make sure that you have your name on both, though, just in case). Also, try to splurge enough to get the exact same size and quality TV

as your primary one. If you can't afford that, make a schedule to alternate who gets to use which TV to avoid any further disputes.

➤ STEP #3: *Throw Out the TV*

If you can't afford two TVs, you might just want to sell the one you have and live without it. Who knows, you might read and have sex a lot more.

➤ STEP #4: *Get Divorced*

If the infighting over the remote doesn't stop, get a divorce or break up and move out. (Make sure you get that f*#!-ing TV in the settlement!)

WHERE THE F*#! IS THE UNIVERSAL, UNIVERSAL REMOTE?

We're not asking for something fancy to control time like in the movie *Click*, just something of manageable size that you can use for your television, your DVD player, your stereo, your thermostat, your microwave oven, the lights, and, of course, to bone your wife.

77. You Find Out Your Girl-friend Is a Stripper

She works late, she's hot, and she knows how to dance really, really sexy. Sometimes she'll see a stop sign when you're walking around town and start twirling around it and dry humping it. But she *says* she's a waitress at a nightclub. Then, one day your friend calls you and thanks you for the lap dance. "Your girlfriend was really good at sitting on my dick and moving around. You didn't tell me she's a stripper."

What now?

The WTF Approach to Dealing with a F*#!-ing Stripper Girlfriend

➤ STEP #1: *Visit Her at Work—Incognito*

If you don't mind the fact that she's a stripper but just want to know whether or not she's actually a hooker too (this may be shocking news, but some strippers are not "just dancing to put themselves through med school"), dress in disguise and visit her place of "business." Buy a lap dance or two and talk in a funny accent. Let her take you to the VIP room and see just how "very important" she makes you feel for a couple hundred bucks.

And then . . .

➤ **OPTION #1: *Break Up with Her***

If you just can't handle that your girlfriend takes off her clothes and sits on stranger's laps until they orgasm—if you are just *that* old-fashioned—you're going to have to break it off. Make sure to at least get a complimentary lap dance for you and all your friends before you call it quits.

➤ **OPTION #2: *Marry Her***

Imagine the possibilities. You could spend the rest of your life having sex with not only her but all her stripper friends—and maybe at the same time. Your so-called marriage will be just one long bachelor party! Plus, when was the last time a stripper *really* wanted you?

➤ **OPTION #3: *Enjoy It While It Lasts***

Chances are good that within a month or two she'll be living at some other guy's house in some other city. Strippers are always on the move. Think of them as naked gypsies that pop a lot of pills and suck a lot of dick.

YOUR GIRLFRIEND MIGHT BE A STRIPPER IF . . .

● She has a tattoo of an arrow pointing to her vagina that says "Pay Here."

● She has a lot of money but it's all in singles.

● She does more coke than Robert Downey Jr.

● She does coke *with* Robert Downey Jr.

What Her Stripper Name Says about Her

● **Candy:** She has an oral fixation and likes to be babied.

● **Danni:** She likes hip-hop, being spanked, and muff diving.

● **Star:** She reads a lot of Stephen Hawking and does a lot of anal.

78. You Forgot Your Girlfriend's Birthday

She seemed a little bitchier than normal, but you chalked it up to PMS. Then she suspiciously asks you the date, but you don't know. You look at the stupid kitty calendar she put up on your wall, and then it hits you in the face. The balloons, the hearts, and the stars covering that little square tell a pretty clear story. But you read the words anyway: "Don't forget my birthday again, or you're a dead man!" You could dump her, admit that you forgot, or tell her that you're now a Jehovah's Witness, but none of these options will help facilitate you getting laid. So here's the plan:

The WTF Approach to Covering Up Forgetting Her F*#!-ing Birthday

> **STEP #1: *Don't Flinch***

Tell her the date, go back to the couch, and keep watching television. While you're watching, try to remember her favorite restaurant and what the hell she might want.

> **STEP #2: *Make Moves***

Excuse yourself to the bathroom for a shower and bring your cell. While the water is running, call the restaurant and make a reservation.

Also, it's time to call in a favor with someone to get a present and flowers delivered there.

➤ STEP #3: *Put Your Plan in Action*

When you get out of the shower, tell her that you're hungry and you want to get a bite to eat. Hopefully, your buddy won't flake.

➤ STEP #4: *Execute*

At the restaurant say, "Happy Birthday." She'll probably be surprised that you remembered. Women love surprises.

IN THE FUTURE . . .

Dump your girlfriends a week or two before their birthdays, Valentine's Day, or Christmas. However much you like her, it's probably going to end soon anyway, so save yourself some money in the process.

If you're not willing to do that, keep a wrapped bottle of fancy chick perfume, a frozen cake, and some champagne in your house. You might as well stock up on tampons, potpourri, Summer's Eve, and Lean Cuisines while you're at it.

79. You Misplaced Your Wedding Ring

As ridiculous and arcane as the tradition of marriage might be, equally ridiculous is the age-old tradition of wearing a wedding ring. Nevertheless, you got married and got a ring. And however you feel about it, if you lose your wedding ring, you better have a damn good excuse.

The WTF Approach to Dealing with a F*#!-ing Misplaced Ring

➤ OPTION #1: *Buy a Replica*

If you've got the cash and you're unlike most married men—in that your wife doesn't go over every single friggin' purchase with a magnifying glass—just cough up the dough and buy another.

➤ OPTION #2: *Cut Off Your Finger*

Though painful, it might pale in comparison to hearing your wife yell at you for what a careless dumbass you are. You can choose to be a real man and just cut it off with a dull knife, or you can get it amputated by a back-alley doctor for a few bucks.

Either way, instead of being yelled at and made to feel guilty and forced to console her, she'll be babying you. Until, of course, she remembers the wedding ring. "Why didn't you find the wedding ring?" she'll say. "If you loved me, you would have made sure to grab it no matter what happened." Women.

➤ OPTION #3: *Cut Off Your Hand*

If you've got a really suspicious wife, then cut off your whole hand. Luckily, it's the left hand—unless, of course, you're unfortunate enough to be left-handed—so it won't hurt your ability to masturbate, which, being married and all, you're definitely going to need.

➤ OPTION #4: *Flip the Switch*

When she asks what happened to your ring, tell her you don't wear it anymore. When she asks why not, just say that you'll start wearing a wedding ring when she starts acting like a wife. After an initial shock, she'll spend the next few weeks wondering what she's done wrong and how to make it up to you. Women.

➤ OPTION #5: *Remove Her Wedding Ring*

Before she notices, remove her wedding ring when she's sleeping. No, don't cut off her hand—that will wake her up. Wait until she's in a deep sleep and rub butter on her finger and slowly slide it off. When she wakes up, she'll probably notice and wonder what happened. At that moment, look down at your hand and say, "Oh my god, mine is gone, too!" This way, you can blame some wedding ring thief that goes into people's houses and steals them.

On the other hand, she might be convinced that your whole marriage was just a dream—or a nightmare.

80. Your Girlfriend Wants to Get Exclusive

This day was bound to come. Where did you think you were, Mars? Who did you think you were, the one guy that can go out with a chick for months and avoid it? Ever been out with a girl before? Did you really think she was just going to go out with you until you were ready to make the next move? Think again, because the time for "the talk" has come. What will your answer be?

The WTF Approach to the F*#!-ing Talk

➤ OPTION #1: *Tell Her You Want to Keep It Open*

If you're not sure whether you want to get serious, nothing will put things in perspective more than the knowledge that she'd be going out with (meaning banging) other guys. If this drives you crazy, then you probably like her and you'll ask *her* to get exclusive.

➤ OPTION #2: *Say, "OK"—but Keep Playing the Field*

The truth of the matter is you never signed up for this, and it's unfair that she alone defines the dynamics of your relationship. You may like her the best out of the women you're dating, but you need more time to see if you want to get exclusive. Make sure you

memorize all phone numbers and take frequent showers.

➤ OPTION #3: *Break It Off*

If you're not *that* into her, break it off now before you cause any more damage. Sure, you'd like to sleep with her for a few more weeks, but bandages are best pulled off quickly. She'll inevitably accuse you of leading her on. Say goodbye and that you're sorry. (Even though you know that in your heart of hearts, you did nothing wrong. You liked her, you went out with her, and you would've liked to keep liking her and going out with her. So WTF is with this woman?)

EVEN IF YOU HAVEN'T HAD "THE TALK," SHE MIGHT THINK YOU'RE EXCLUSIVE IF:

- You go out with her every Saturday night.

- You've met her family more than once.

- She keeps a lot of her crap at your house.

- You've been dating more than a month.

- You pick her up and/or drop her off at the airport.

- You've taken her on more than one weekend trip.

- You've helped her move.

NOTE: While none of these things constitutes an implicit exclusive dating agreement, a few together may. However, if she keeps a box of tampons in your bathroom cabinet, you've definitely got a girlfriend. And before you know it, a wife, too.

there goes the
neighborhood

81. You Are Accosted by Proselytizers

Most religious groups try to woo new members. It's just the way it is. And their intentions are usually good. They are, after all, trying to save your soul. But while the motives may be admirable, these pushy proselytizers can be a bit annoying, especially when you've just laid down to take a nap after a long day at work and they keep ringing your doorbell like some cheap door-to-door salespeople. And then they start with the questioning, "Have you ever heard of the Church of Latter Day Saints?" What do they think you are, an idiot? Of course you've heard of Mormons. How couldn't you? They stop by every other week, for Christ's sake!

The WTF Approach to Handling F*#!-ing Proselytizers

►**OPTION #1:** *Answer the Door in a Devil's Costume*

It's good to keep some Halloween Satan horns and a pitchfork lying around so that when unexpected and unwelcome missionaries come pounding on your door, you can scare the crap out of them. Just look through your peephole to make sure that you're dealing with proselytizers and not the little kid next door. It's not hard to spot

them: Look for the pontific smiles, cheap suits, and the subtle gaze of wasted youth.

> OPTION #2: *Flip the Switch*

Two can play at the proselytizing game. Let them in and hear what they have to say. After listening intently as if you might be interested, break out some of your own literature on the religion of your choice—like satanic transsexual worshipping, for instance. After having listened so politely to their spiel, they'll feel compelled to hear you out. Try to waste as much of their time as possible, just like they had planned to do with you.

> OPTION #3: *Try to Seduce Them*

This will (most likely) *not* work out, but it will make sure that these proselytizers won't come back. And if they do, you know what they're back for. They want to get to know you . . . in the biblical sense.

PROGRESS IN PROSELYTIZING

Fanatical proselytizers are, in this country at least, at worst, just annoying. Not that long ago, saying "no" to a conversion didn't end with a polite, but admonishing, "God bless your soul"—it ended with them tying you up and setting you on fire.

Heaven Is a Restaurant

Think of your favorite television evangelist as the maître d' at a restaurant called Heaven's. How much you donate determines where you get to sit. Here's a breakdown:

$100	Sit at the bar
$1,000	Get a shitty table in the back
$10,000	Great table with good view of Jesus
$100,000	Seat at a table with Jesus
$1,000,000	Sit on Jesus' lap

82. Your Best Friend Is Still on Your Couch

When Vinnie told you he was moving to your town, you were ecstatic. It was like old times! But now it's getting old. When one month became two months, you shrugged your shoulders. When two months became five months, you clenched your teeth. You're now in one of the most awkward situations in life. Your best friend won't leave your couch, and he ain't paying to stay on it.

The WTF Approach to Getting That F*#!-ing Bum Off Your Couch

➤ STEP #1: *Question Him*

Ask him what his plans are, and how the job search is going. If you're uncomfortable being direct, be sure to pepper those questions with: How do you like it here so far? Have you made any new friends? What area do you like best?

➤ STEP #2: *Encourage Him*

Your friend seems to have motivation issues, so get involved. Help him fix his resume and look for apartments. Maybe he hasn't yet found a job where he can best apply his many God-given talents. Perhaps he can find a job eating cereal all day as some kind of

product tester. Or since he likes the couch so much, maybe he has a future in the furniture business. Spend a little time mentoring him to help him get on his feet. He ain't gonna do it by himself.

➤ STEP #3: *Give Him a Deadline*

You've tried being subtle, you've tried being helpful, but neither has worked. It's time to talk eviction dates.

➤ STEP #4: *Find Him a Girlfriend*

The unfortunate truth is that some guys don't do shit unless a girl tells them to. Find him a lonely, desperate, generous woman with a mommy complex to take care of him. Now he's her problem, not yours. You can find these women *anywhere*.

➤ STEP #5: *Learn to Live with It*

Let's face it. You're never going to kick him out. The deadline has come and gone—twice. He's your best friend. But if he ain't going to pay rent, he's going to have to pay in other ways. Make him clean up his shit—and yours. Make him do the laundry, the dishes, and scrub your bathroom until it's so clean you could eat off it. Then, make him eat off it.

Interpreting Couch Potato Speak

He says: "I applied to ten jobs on craigslist."
He means: *"I applied to one job, jerked off, took a nap, and jerked off again."*
He says: "I saw about five apartments."
He means: *"I drove by a few for-rent signs on the way to the pub."*
He says: "I met this really great chick and she was way into me."
He means: *"The barista smiled at me."*

83. You Got a Dog Trainer and Your Dog Still Pees on the Floor

Your heart was in the right place when you bought the little, cute four-legged pain in the ass. And you thought you were doing the right thing by forking out the cash for a trainer, but now you're still finding yourself knee-deep in dog shit in your own house. If you can't seem to housebreak the monster, try our tips.

The WTF Approach to Dealing with a F*#!-ing Piss-Happy Puppy

➤ OPTION #1: *Call Cesar Milan*

You got screwed by an amateur—now it's time to call in the pro. Known as the "Dog Whisperer," Milan is a famous dog trainer who will turn the most untamable canine into Lassie. To sign up to be a guest on his hit show *The Dog Whisperer,* just look him up on Google. You can find your own link, bozo, you don't need us.

➤ OPTION #2: *Buy a Doghouse*

Just keep the dog outside at all times or in a doghouse. Snoopy had to live that way, for Christ's sake, why can't Fido?

➤ OPTION #3: *An Unfortunate "Accident"*

If you don't want to break your kid's heart (or at least not be held

responsible for doing so), kill the puppy, but make it look like an accident. Here's how:

Kill all the dogs in the 'hood: This idea won't make it look like an accident, but it will take the suspicion off you. Plus, it would allow your kid to join other grieving kids on the block and draw strength from one another. And, it will make the neighborhood more peaceful—once the wails and moans of grieving children quiet down.

Poison the puppy: You can use just about anything in large amounts. Yes, rat poison works for dogs, too.

Let the dog out: Carefully take the puppy's leash off your child's sleeping arm and let the puppy out so you can later blame your confused, sobbing kid for not watching it. Chances are, it will die out there. This experience will also serve to teach little Billy about the importance of responsibility. Not to mention, you can look like a hero by keeping your cool in the face of his incredible lack of responsibility.

WTF: UP CLOSE AND PERSONAL

Any dog can live outside. Take my uncle's Alaskan Husky. When Uncle Bob bought a new house, he wanted to keep it nice and didn't want to get dog fur everywhere. So he built a beautiful, luxurious doghouse in the big backyard.

Bob happened to live in Phoenix, where temperatures can reach 130 degrees. The dog may not have been predisposed to that kind of heat, being from Alaska and all, but Bob's house sure was gorgeous.

—AWH

REMEMBERING RODNEY

" Some dog I got, too. We call him Egypt. Because in every room he leaves a pyramid. "

—Rodney Dangerfield

84. The Cops Show Up at Your House Party

There's nothing that spoils the mood of a nice, quiet, debaucherous get-together more than the po'. When your neighbors finally get sick of all the noise, they won't hesitate to call the cops. But that doesn't mean the party's over, as long as you follow our step-by-step guide.

The WTF Approach to Survive a F*#!-ing Party-Crashing

➤ STEP #1: *Turn Down the Loud Music*

Nine times out of ten, the cops are there because of a noise complaint. Close your windows, use your inside voices, and keep the music down.

➤ STEP #2: *Hide the Evidence*

Get anything illegal out of sight. This includes: drugs, underage girls, buddies who skipped out on parole, and hookers. Send them down to the basement or into the bathroom, stat.

➤ STEP #3: *Don't Answer the Door*

Police need a warrant and they're not getting one in the middle of the night. If they do come in, you can meet them in court. A loud noise does not constitute grounds for probable cause. And the worst that can happen if you try to ignore them is they come in anyway.

Not Invited?

Never get invited to house parties? Then call the cops on the cool kids and shut down their fun. Say that you're their neighbor and that you've asked them to be quiet and they won't. Say that you have seen them doing narcotics, and you believe there are underage kids there. Also, say that you have reason to believe that the party is really the meeting place of a violent, antigovernment group that harbors a particular hatred of local police.

IN THE FUTURE . . .

Keep the cops away by keeping your dirtbag friends off your lawn. No one likes to see a bunch of creeps drinking cans of Pabst in their neighborhood. Bring them inside.

Also, don't let any anyone in who's more than two degrees of separation from you. You're buddy's brother is fine. But his friend is not. This way you keep down fights, thefts, and vomiting. Although, if it's a really hot chick, f*#! the rules.

85. Your New House Is Infested with Termites

As you toured the house before the sale, you wondered what all those little particles were on the kitchen floor, but dismissed them for dust and crumbs. It wasn't until you moved in and saw one of the buggers did you realize, "Yep. That's termite shit." Well, here's what to do:

The WTF Approach to Getting Rid of F*#!-ing Termites

➤ OPTION #1: *Call the Exterminator*

If you're lucky, he'll put a bug circus tent over your house. Don't forget to take your pets—and your kids—to the hotel with you. If you really need the cash, you can hire a clown to stand out front to try to get kids to go in.

➤ OPTION #2: *Sell Them to Africa*

Fried termites are considered a tasty snack in Africa. Selling off your nasty pests will not only make a little kid over there happy when he gets a handful of yummy bugs, as an export it will help offset our massive trade deficit.

➤ OPTION #3: *Eat Them Yourself*

Termites are a good source of fat and protein, and have a nice nutty flavor when cooked. Yum!

➤ OPTION #4: *Learn to Live with Them*

Feed your termites scraps of wood and learn to communicate with them by wiggling your ears.

➤ OPTION #5: *Move*

Pretend you never saw the little bastards and sell your house to some other schmuck.

WTFACT: Termites cost Americans more than $1 billion each year. So, if you see one, step on it.

86. Someone's Growing Marijuana on Your Property

M any people have a soft spot in their heart for pot. But that doesn't mean you want to play Waco with the feds or get caught in a gang war. So when you come across a secret stash of dank being raised on your property, it's best to know all the potential hazards of your next move.

The WTF Approach to Dealing with a F*#!-ing Hidden Pot Garden

➤ OPTION #1: *Call the Cops*

This is the most logical option, unless you think whoever put the weed there might come after you for the money. So know your neighborhood and get a shotgun.

➤ OPTION #2: *Throw a Party*

If you're looking for a good time, a giant party might be just what you need to solve your pot-garden problem, your no-friend problem, and your need-to-get-laid problem all at once. If some free green can't help you, you'll have to trade it for massage parlor services.

➤ OPTION #3: *Enter the Record Books*

Fly in the bozos from *Guinness*, use all that weed to roll the biggest blunt ever, and become

immortalized. You'll share space with athletes, politicians, humanitarians, and the guy with the longest fingernails. Good work!

➤ OPTION #4: *Start Dealing*

Though you never dreamed of getting into the drug trade, you don't miss an opportunity when it falls in your lap. It's a riskier but much more lucrative venture, and you'll want to make sure whoever planted it isn't coming back. Once your dealers hit the streets, your competition is going to start wondering where all that bud came from. You'll need a small posse of gun-toting cowboys to keep the banditos away.

WHERE TO SELL THE GANJA

- College campuses
- Medical-marijuana distribution sites
- ~~High schools~~
- Rock concerts

- Video game conventions
- ~~Elementary schools~~
- Local parks
- ~~Kindergartens~~

> **NOTE:** If you think your operation is going to be an easy street of laughs like *Weeds*, think again. You're going to be involving yourself in some *Wire*-type shit. Don't say we didn't warn you.

➤ OPTION #5: *Burn It*

F*#! the police. F*#! drugs. F*#! Jerry Garcia. Make it look like someone threw a cigarette out of their car window and torch the shit. This way, no one can blame you. You didn't know anything about it. You didn't tell the cops. And you'll get the whole damn town as high as a kite.

. . . But do you think you could grab an ounce for your two favorite authors before you do it? We have glaucoma, swear to Chong. Come on dude, WTF?

87. Your Parish Priest Is Accused of Child Molestation

Turns out, Father O'Brien was really Father O'BlowJob.

The WTF Approach to F*#!-ing Kiddy-Diddling Priests

➤ STEP #1: *Don't Feel Slighted*

You were a good-looking kid, with hair as pale as wheat, with eyes as blue as the sea, and with delicate features, chiseled to perfection by the hand of God. Any servant of the Lord would've been lucky to have you bowed on your knees before him.

➤ STEP #2: *Don't Move*

Stay where you are, because before you know it, he'll be transferred to another parish, with the full support of the Catholic Church, to tend to a new flock of kids.

➤ STEP #3: *Pray for Him*

If your faith in the Church hasn't been tarnished, pray for him. After all, he's simply a glorious servant of God who, seduced by the devil, has taken the wrong path.

➤ STEP #4: *Become a Real Catholic*

You know, the kind that only goes to church on Easter and shows her tits at Mardi Gras. The kind that skips church during football season, as well as baseball season, basketball season, hockey season, and NASCAR season. If you aren't

in church, you're not going to have a problem with sicko priests.

Or . . .

➤ STEP #4: *Convert*

Maybe Luther was right, after all. And if you're worried about any funny business going on with Protestants, don't. They're only interested in one kind of coming: The Second Coming.

HOW TO STOP PRIESTS FROM SEXUAL ASSAULT

- Castrate them. They aren't supposed to use it for anything other than pissing, anyway.

- Require them to get married. Maybe the ability to get laid will keep the creeps out of the seminaries.

- Hold more nun/priest mixers.

- Stop moving them to another Parish when they get caught diddling kids!

It Happens in All Religions

Ask any Catholic about the ubiquity of child molestation in the Catholic Church and you get the same answer: "It happens in all religions. You just hear more about it in Catholicism." Really? You really believe that rabbis are playing hide the challah with young boys at synagogues across America? You know they aren't. That goes for Muslim and Protestant religions too, no matter how fanatical. And say what you want about how nuts Tom Cruise and his Scientologist cronies are, but at least they're not raping boys. Cruise gets to bed women like Nicole Kidman, Penelope Cruise, and his new plaything, that *Dawson's Creek* chick—who does kind of look like a boy, come to think of it . . .

WTFACT: In 1992, a nonprofit organization was founded in Australia to help victims of church-related sexual abuse. The organization has reported that approximately 90 percent of the victims who have contacted them have been Catholic. About 25 percent of the country is Catholic. Need we say more?

88. Your Dog Knocks Up Your Neighbor's Dog

Man's best friend can't be much smarter than his master. All those times he's watched you ride bareback has apparently rubbed off on him. Then, one day, your neighbor comes over with an ugly little pregnant bitch and claims that your Fido is the daddy. But don't fret, and don't throw Fido under the bus quite yet.

The WTF Approach to Handling Your F*#!-ing Fertile Pooch

> **STEP #1: *Don't Admit Anything,* Ever**

Just like when you crashed your car, drank too much and got into a fight, or fathered your first illegitimate child, don't admit guilt. It's not for you to decide. It's for lawyers, judges, insurance agents, and ultimately God to figure out.

> **STEP #2: *Blame the Bitch***

"You know she wanted it, she's such a slut. Always sniffing Fido's ass." If you say it straight, your neighbor will never bother you again. Nor will he ever let his kids outside.

➤ STEP #3: *Offer to Help*

Without accepting any responsibility, tell your neighbor that you'll be more than happy to take care of the puppies once they're born, no matter who screwed his pootch. You'll take care of them, all right—by burying them alive in the backyard.

HOW TO TELL IF YOUR DOG IS SLEEPING AROUND:

- When you went to work, there was one dog food bowl; when you came home, there were two.

- He used to squirm when you took him to the groomer's; now he gets excited.

- The vet always gave him a clean bill of health. Now he tells you Fido has AIDS.

Neuter the Little Bastard

Do like Bob Barker always said and whack off his nuts. If you still believe that you might one day breed him, get your head examined and then whack off his nuts. People who breed dogs live on farms, not in condos. They have kennels, not duct tape and sticks. And, they know much more about dogs than how much weed it takes to get 'em stoned. If you're a weirdo and think that a dog without balls is embarrassing, you can pay an extra few bucks and get plastic gonads installed. It's worth it. Would you want to walk around with an empty sack?

WTFACT: Every year, animal shelters kill about 5 million dogs. Not only is that brutal, it's expensive and your taxes pay for all the cages, drugs, and vets. Don't be a bozo, chop off Fido's nuts.

89. You Accidentally Run Over Your Neighbor's Dog

Dogs are great. They're our loyal companions and our best friends—we even consider them members of our family. Despite that, they're stupid. They chase their own tails, eat their own shit, and enjoy nothing more than the smell of your crotch. So don't feel too bad when you turn your neighbor's golden retriever into a pile of bloody meat. You may have been speeding, on the phone, and only half watching the road, but it's not really your fault. He should have looked both ways.

The WTF Approach to Dealing with a Dead F*#!-ing Dog

➤ STEP #1: *Make Sure It's Dead*

If it's not dead already, it's going to be pissed and bite the shit out of you. Do the humane thing and throw your car in reverse.

NOTE: If there's a sensitive person in your car—like a woman, child, or vegetarian—she might try to persuade you to help the dog. Don't. Even if it doesn't bite you, you'll get blood on your clothes and your upholstery, the vet will charge you $500, your neighbor will hate you, and the dog will still die.

➤ STEP #2: *Order Chinese Takeout*

Relax and treat yourself to a little sweet and sour pork and a nice cup of wonton soup. After all, you've had a hard day—you just killed a puppy. Eat your fortune cookie and then move its carcass over to your neighbor's porch in the cover of night.

➤ STEP #3: *Make Up for It*

Donate a couple bucks to the local SPCA or adopt a puppy from impending eternal sleep.

➤ STEP #4: *Compensate for Their Loss*

Your neighbors are no doubt torn up about the passing of their pooch—not to mention finding its bloodied remains on their porch.

Grab a DVD you don't watch anymore, hand it to your neighbor, and say, "Sorry for your loss."

➤ STEP #5: *All Dogs Go to Heaven*

Don't beat yourself up over this. Most of these mutts don't even work for a living. Their jobs are to lie around and eat all day. Then they get sent off to heaven where they chase mailmen and sit on the couch. Overall, it's a far better life than yours.

WTFACT: Estimates put the number of dogs in the world at 400 million. There are more dogs in the world than there are people in the United States and each country of the world except for China and India.

90. You Think a Terrorist Just Moved into Your Neighborhood

In these troubled times, it's best to be extra careful. This is especially true when it comes to our families and our homes. When someone with an accent moves in next door, it's only natural to get a little anxious. Because of what's on the news, it may be tempting to only worry if the new neighbor is Middle Eastern, but that shouldn't be the case. According to the U.S. National Counterterrorism Center, only 21 percent of terrorism is perpetrated by Islamic extremists and more than half, a full 59 percent, is committed by unknown people with unknown motives. Be afraid—of everyone.

It's about time we add Nepalese Communists, Basque Separatists, and the Irish Republican Army—among many, many others—to our list of who to watch. Terrorists are white, black, and yellow. They're communist, anti-communist, and anti-anti-communist.

But there's one thing for sure. There's no way in hell they're moving in next to your family.

The WTF Approach to Your F*#!-ing Friendly Neighborhood Terrorist

> **STEP #1: *Organize***

Gather a group of concerned citizens and form a neighborhood terror watch. Post stickers on the windows of all participants' homes, allowing terrorists to know that their ideas, their way of life, and their bombs are not welcome in your community.

> **STEP #2: *Demonstrate***

Luckily, the first amendment allows for peaceable demonstrations of any point of view. A demonstration could make your would-be terrorists think twice about moving in next to such concerned, proactive citizens.

> **STEP #3: *Fight Fire with Fire***

While we can't condone illegal acts, nothing gets terrorists out of the neighborhood as quickly as a house fire. Remember: Nothing fights terrorism better than counter-terrorism, which is always completely different and justifiable.

Is Your Son an Islamic Terrorist?

Forget about the boy next door—what about the boy upstairs? "The American Taliban" John Walker proved that anyone's kid might turn into an Islamic terrorist. Here are some signs that your son might be on the way toward dangerous fanaticism.

YOUR SON MIGHT BE AN ISLAMIC EXTREMIST IF . . .

- He used to eat hamburger. Now he eats lamburger.

- He used to watch *Girls Gone Wild*. Now he watches *Girls Gone Burqa*.

- He used to smoke a bong. Now he smokes a hookah.

- He used to ride a skateboard. Now he rides a camel.

- He used to dream of sluts. Now he dreams of virgins.

But again, you can't just look for telltale signs of Islamic terrorism—there are other terrorist groups your son might fall prey to.

YOUR SON MIGHT BE AN IRA MEMBER IF . . .

- He used to love apple pie. Now he loves shepherd's pie.

- He used to complain about his teachers. Now he complains about the British.

- He used to love soda. Now he loves soda bread.

- He used to bang cheerleaders. Now he bangs leprechauns.

- He used to read *SI*, *The Onion*, and *Rolling Stone*. Now he reads Joyce, Yeats, and Heaney.

YOUR SON MIGHT BE A NEPALESE COMMUNIST IF . . .

- He used to use a graphing calculator for his advanced algebra class. Now he uses an abacus.

- He used to drive around town in his convertible. Now he rides a yak.

- He used to go for walks in the park to get fresh air. Now he climbs on the roof.

YOUR SON MIGHT BE A BASQUE SEPARATIST IF . . .

- He used to eat anything. Now he refuses to eat tapas.

- He used to have a picture of President Bush on his dartboard. Now it's a picture of Franco.

- He used to watch *So You Think You Can Dance*. Now the flamenco makes him cringe.

tech troubles

91. Your Girlfriend Demands You Cut Back on the Internet Porn

Sometimes pornography seems infinitely more appealing than even the prospect of a woman. It's cheaper, there's less mess, and *you* always know exactly what you want. But that doesn't mean she's okay with you always opting for the e-porn. A healthy person should have a mix of porn and real women—but probably more porn. But still, you're going to have to learn how to cut back.

The WTF Approach to Beating Your F*#!-ing e-Beating

➤ STEP #1: *Block It Out*

Get a babysitter program for your computer and just smash keys like this— oeruwgfc3iuewacwqpoi— for your password. Or, call your Internet provider and have it block words like "interracial," "gang-bang," and "facial."

If, for some reason, you have to write an essay on the social impact of interracial marriage, the growing influence of gangs in the inner city, or new techniques in personal beauty, go to the library, where jerking off is frowned upon.

Nowadays, there's no social element to masturbation. Whatever happened to hanging out on 42nd Street, drinking a beer out of a bag, having a couple of smokes, talking to your buddies, and then excusing yourself to go into the booth and jerk off all over the floor. Peep shows, coin booths, and porno theaters weren't just places to get off, they were an indelible part of urban social life . . . a great place to meet interesting new friends—*and* jerk off.

➤ STEP #2: *Hang a Giant Crucifix Above Your Monitor*

Even if you're not particularly religious, this should turn you off from trying to access your porn— unless you're into bondage.

➤ STEP #3: *Go Old School*

Wean yourself off Internet porn by buying DVDs. Once the cravings subside, toss the DVDs, and buy a couple of dirty magazines.

THE SEVEN LEVELS OF PORN ADDICTION

I: You stay up late every night to look at porn.

II: You look at porn at work.

III: You turn down sex to look at porn. (But not if you're married—that's not addiction, that's marriage.)

IV: You keep asking your girlfriend if she's into gangbangs.

V: You've erased your favorite songs from your iPod to make room for all your favorite pornos—so you can watch them *wherever* you go.

VI: You bring a girl back from the bar and expect her to do double penetration with you and your parakeet.

VII: You stop banging your girlfriend altogether.

92. Your Bank Account Is Hacked Into

It's a disease of the information age. Cyberdorks do stupid shit online all day long. At some point, they come to the conclusion that they should stop coding dumb games and living in their momma's basement. So they start hacking into bank accounts, and today they just hit yours.

The WTF Approach to a F*#!-ing Internet Hijacking

➤ STEP #1: *Go into the Bank*

Waiting twenty minutes in line beats waiting five days on the phone.

➤ STEP #2: *Blame the Bank*

Remember, even if you're less than vigilant when it comes to account security, never admit it's your fault. Bankers are some of the cheapest, meanest, greediest people in the world, and you don't want to give them any reason not to give you back your cash

➤ STEP #3: *Stop Banking Online*

The Internet is as perilous as it is convenient. You can satisfy most of your banking needs by using the ATM.

➤ STEP #4: *Stop Banking Altogether*

You don't trust bankers, so why do business with them? Those suits are just there to steal your hard-earned money. Put your cash in your cowboy hat and slip it under the bed.

93. Your Homemade Sex Tape Winds Up Online

While celebrities such as Pamela Anderson and Paris Hilton may have been sincerely disappointed by the release of their most private moments to the public, it significantly improved both of their careers.

That said, your career in corporate communications is probably not going to get a boost if this happens to you. That is, unless you performed much better than either one of those ladies did, which wouldn't be hard to do. (Sorry, ladies, we weren't that impressed—especially you, Paris. Now, the guys on the other hand, well, that's a different story.)

The WTF Approach to Seeing Yourself on F*#!-ing YouPorn

➤ STEP #1: *Who Done It?*

If an ex uploaded the video, you have every right to kick his—or her—ass. It's one thing to masturbate to that digital trip down memory lane, but it's another to let the whole world get off on it. Now you'll never know if that attractive stranger across the bar is smiling at you because you're hot or if it's

because she's seen a video of you begging for it like a dog in heat.

➤ STEP #2: *Wait It Out*

Luckily, however, there's so much porn online now that the chances of anyone you know running into your video is probably slim, unless you're both into some wacky fetish. And if that's the case, you probably don't mind.

WTFACT: About one out of every ten websites are porn and about 250 new sites are being added to the list of porn websites daily. So, the chances your mom will run across your video are not good. But when your pervert brother finds it, he'll be sure to let her know—after he whacks off, and, stricken with a sense of overwhelming guilt, cries uncontrollably.

➤ STEP #3: *Learn from It*

Just be happy you're not with her anymore. It's been a while, and you forgot what a hideous body she had. At least that will assure that the lifespan of this video will be much shorter than the herpes you gave her.

➤ STEP #4: *Milk It*

No, not *that*; you already did that. We're talking about the video. Ride your wave of porno success and start your own website. Start filming every time you get busy with a new friend—but be sure to check IDs. Monetize the site. Now you can say you're an entrepreneur with a technology company—even though you're really just a ho with a camera.

IN THE FUTURE . . .

Promise you'll never look like that again. Can you believe how you wore your hair back then? God, how embarrassing. Never go back to that style.

94. Your Computer Breaks Down and You're on a Deadline

When your computer breaks, the prospect of buying a new one can be daunting—and like most daunting tasks, you want to put it off. But you're on deadline, you lazy son of a bitch, so put your ass in gear and buy a new one. Yes, you'll have a lot of options to choose from, and yes, it's a lot of money, but it's essential. We know, all you want to do is get back to how it was before the meltdown, when you could merrily watch your favorite TV shows and porn at the same time—after you finished your report, of course.

The WTF Approach to Replacing Your F*#!-ing Computer

> **STEP #1:** *Don't Trust Anything a Salesperson Tells You*

Sorry, bud, you're going to have to do your own research. The salesperson is there to sell. He's not there to give you a good deal. Even if he isn't working off commission, his salary is tied to his sales.

> **STEP #2:** *Don't Just Buy Anything*

It saves you a lot of hassle to just walk in to the store and grab the first thing that will work, but these aren't socks. Be choosey.

➤ STEP #3: *Don't Believe Your Friends*

Unless your friend is a computer engineer, he's probably just as stupid as you are.

➤ STEP #4: *Don't Buy a Warranty*

They're just a way for the store to get another couple hundred bucks out of you because you're afraid. If you want to gamble, bet on yourself, not against yourself.

➤ STEP #5: *Get Your Old Files Recovered*

Take your old computer to a geek, and pay whatever it takes to get your data. You may have to sell your car or get a second mortgage, but at least you won't be canned.

How Much Should You Spend on a Computer?

A computer costs as much as you want to spend. Want one that's able to shoot a missile at another missile in the stratosphere? That'll be several billion bucks. Want one that'll let you look at porn and send e-mails to chicks around your town? Don't spend more than $500. Also, don't buy any software. You should be able to get everything you need from a friend or free on the Internet.

95. Your Connection Goes Down in the Middle of Warcraft

Oh my God! What's happening? I can't get online! I can't get online! My level 70 Blood Elf Paladin is going to die! My guild is going to be pissed! Someone help! I can't get online! *Aaaaaaahhhhhhhh*!!!

Relax. There is a world outside of cyberspace.

The WTF Approach to a F*#!-ing Broken Internet Connection

➤ OPTION #1: *Fix It*

Unless you're a big-time techie, fixing it requires about two days. One day is spent on hold waiting for a "technician," and another is spent troubleshooting with this "technician."

➤ OPTION #2: *Move to a Café*

Internet cafes are great because it's just like being at home, except the muffins are better and the coffee costs five bucks.

➤ OPTION #3: *Don't Fix It*

Do something else for once. It may seem like living without one foot in cyberspace is equivalent to living like a caveman, but it isn't. Remember, you first got hooked up to the web in 1999—not 1979.

Alternatives to Being Online

Real life may seem more dull and trying than you remember. If you need ideas about what to do, try looking at the Yellow Pages, which is probably wrapped in cellophane under your sofa. Or try out some of these ideas:

Chat face to face: Instead of chatting with your buddy in Beijing, try chatting with your friend down the street—and I don't mean with a webcam. While he may not be into rare projectile weaponry of the Ming Dynasty like your pal who you met in a chat room of the same name, the "life-like" and animated quality of a face-to-face conversation might make up for it. It seems so real.

Go to a porno theatre: Can't get your kicks online? Visit an old-fashioned theater that features pornographic films. If you have specific fetishes, such as goats in high heels ridden by nude midgets, you might be disappointed

with what these relics of the 1970s have to offer. After all, who can get off to two people just having sex anymore?

MAJOR CONTRIBUTIONS TO COMPUTING AND INTERNET TECHNOLOGY
IBM
Xerox
Microsoft
Apple
Al Gore

Go to an arcade: Remember the old days when you would go to an arcade with your friends to play Pac-Man and it was the most fun you could ever have? Relive that fun time. Beware, however, that for the good games, it's about $3.50 a pop. Oh, and do us a favor, beat the shit out of those kids making an ass out of themselves on Dance, Dance Revolution while you're there.

Pick up a newspaper: Get your news somewhere other than *Yahoo.com*. Marvel at the anachronistic black and white coloring and the feel of the paper between your fingertips. Relish that moment. They'll soon be gone.

96. You Keep Losing Your Cell Phone

These days, technology is making our lives more convenient. Cell phones are rapidly becoming smaller, faster, and more advanced. But there's one feature these gadgets seem to be missing: a feature that prevents you from losing the f*#!-ing thing.

The WTF Approach to Keeping Track of Your F*#!-ing Cell Phone

➤ OPTION #1: *Back It Up*

Keep all your important numbers and information not just on the hard drive of your computer or on a jump drive, but in a spiral notebook under your bed. Even if you're accident prone, losing your bed is difficult.

➤ OPTION #2: *Wear It as a Necklace*

You may think it looks stupid, but it's certainly practical. Not only that—if you're otherwise cool enough, you could rock it and make it work. God knows, there have been stupider fads, such as leaving the price tag on a baseball cap. If that can be popular, why can't wearing a Motorola around your neck?

➤ OPTION #3: *Get a Part-Time Job with Nokia*

Even successful professionals take part-time jobs at Starbucks for the health insurance. Work a few hours a week there. They could offer deep discounts on phones. Call them to find out. Make sure to put your phone back around your neck when you're done, bozo.

➤ OPTION #4: *Buy the Most Expensive Cell Phone There Is*

If you pay $50 for a phone, you might not pay too much attention to it. But if you pay $5,000 for a phone, you won't forget about it for a second.

➤ OPTION #5: *Go Old School*

Get a land line and an answering machine. These days they're dirt cheap. If you want to talk on the go, get the longest extension cord you can find. It may look stupid, but it's better than tying a phone around your neck, putz.

WTF: UP CLOSE AND PERSONAL

I speak from experience here. I've lost twelve phones in twelve months. Literally a phone a month. FYI, insurance plans only cover two phones per year. Unfortunately, all the proceeds of this book will go to financing my expensive cell-phone-losing habit. FYI, I am a moron.

—GB

WHAT THE F*#! IS UP WITH . . . CONSTANT COMMUNICATION

It used to be easy to avoid people. Just let the message machine pick up and that was it. But with the advent of cell phones, all of a sudden, everyone became as reachable as a doctor on call. But even cell phones can be turned off, and you could always say that you couldn't get a signal. But not now. With text messaging and e-mail functions, avoiding people without arousing suspicion is virtually impossible. I guess you're going to have to just be honest and tell them you hate them once and for all. If you're a coward, text them.

97. Your Inbox Is Overloaded with Spam and Crashes

Spammers are the scum of the universe. With thousands and thousands of these pricks sending penis-enlargement plans, weight loss options, and hot stock tips every day, fighting them is going to be a losing battle. Here are some tips that just might put a dent in the amount of spam you get.

The WTF Approach to Avenging Your F*#!-ing Inbox

> ➤ STEP #1: *Get a Spam-Blocking Program*

There are dozens of quality programs that will reduce the amount of spam that gets into your inbox. You've got enough penile enlargement pills to last you years, anyway.

> ➤ STEP #2: *Never Reply to Spam*

That just tells the spammers that your e-mail address is a good one to send shit to.

> ➤ STEP #3: *Never Make a Purchase Based on a Spam*

This makes spam campaigns effective. Punish anyone who uses spam to get them to stop.

➤ STEP #4: *Change Your E-mail Address*

If spam gets too overwhelming, change everything. Change your name, your apartment, and your sex. This *should* stop you from getting all that penile-enhancement spam, but we all know that it won't.

➤ STEP #5: *Tattle!*

Report the spam to the appropriate authorities. If you can't unsubscribe, it violates CAN-SPAM. If you get spam that you think is deceptive, forward it to spam@uce.gov. The Federal Trade Commission uses the spam stored in that database to pursue law enforcement actions against people who send deceptive e-mail. If it has a stock ticker, the Securities and Exchange Commission probably wants that address. Forward investment-related spam to enforcement@sec.gov. Since these are government agencies, they might take up to a decade to do anything, if they ever do anything.

Also tell Google, Yahoo, MSN, and anyone else you feel like. These are the real Internet cops (and robbers).

Our Favorite Spam

It's nice when spammers get a little creative instead of just being annoying. This one stood out and became a favorite.

"At last you've met a gal that's hot
You wanna hump her moistened twat.
She's full of passion, she's so nice!
But would your penile size suffice?
Not sure she will ask for more?
You need a wang she would adore!
But how to get it long and thick?
Your only hope is MegaDik!
You'll get so wanted super-size
And see great pleasure in her eyes!
Your shaft will pound her poon so deep,
Tonight you'll hardly fall asleep!
So try today this magic p'ill
And change your life at your own will!"
—Courtesy of an email from jody@ms46.hinet.net

98. You Have to Open Another Flickr Account Because You Took So Many Damn Pictures

They say a picture is worth a thousand words. The reason they said that was because taking a picture used to be a pain in the ass. Between carrying and setting up the equipment and all the time in the darkroom, taking a picture wasn't easy. This long process meant that pictures weren't taken thoughtlessly. A "Kodak Moment" was something out of the ordinary—a moment worth capturing.

Now, in the digital age, you can take a picture effortlessly, post it online, and share it with friends at virtually no cost. People today take a picture of about every goddamn thing they do. "My new cool toothbrush," "Look, I'm wearing pants, dude," "OMG, I'm out having a drink with a friend I see five times a week." A thousand words, really?

It's OK. You can admit you're one of "those" people. You're among friends and we're here to help—even lame people like you.

The WTF Approach to Kicking Your F*#!-ing Photo Habit

> **STEP #1:** *Take a Class*

Photography is an art form, just like painting, sculpture, or writing humor books. Learn to appreciate the art form and pick your subjects—and your moments—more critically. With this new appreciation, you won't take a picture of your friend taking a piss outside a bar, unless you use a set of specific aesthetic guidelines and put it into a social perspective.

> **STEP #2:** *Leave It at Home*

If you're not traveling, seeing a friend you haven't seen in years, or witnessing a crime, you really need to ask yourself if this moment is worth capturing forever.

> **STEP #3:** *Just Have Fun*

Stop thinking that you have to document every smile. If you go out to some place with friends and want to take a picture, fine. Take *one*. Have everyone gather around and take a picture. That's all you need, so you can go back later and say "Oh, remember when . . . ." A hundred pictures aren't necessary.

> **STEP #4:** *Stop Sharing Photos*

If you *really* can't help yourself: Take all the pictures you want, but stop *sharing* them. If you really think everyone wants to see 400 pictures of you and your friends at the mall, you need to see a specialist. They don't. No one does.

for the ladies . . .

If you want to take a thousand pictures every time you leave the house, fine—just leave us men the f*#! out of it. We'll take our own. Like when Chris fell off his motorcycle and his feet were pointing the wrong way. Or our trip to Bangkok we never told you about. You would have been proud. We took *a lot* of pictures.

99. Some Creep Is Cyberstalking You

He's poked you on Facebook, messaged you on MySpace, and sent you an IM on AIM, all with creepy details about your personal likes and dislikes and daily life. But you haven't a damn idea who this person could be. Well now you do—he's your very own cyberstalker.

If your information is on the Internet, you're open to cyberstalking. Your cyberstalker could be an ex-girlfriend, an old classmate, or a sick murderer/pervert out to get you. No matter what, getting cyberstalked is f*#!-ing creepy. Here are some tips to avoid these creeps.

The WTF Approach to F*#!-ing Cyberstalkers

➤ STEP #1: *Keep a Low Profile*

Don't publish your phone number, e-mail address, or physical address. Cyberstalkers can search for you in any city in the country. Keep your MySpace page private as well. You don't need potential cyberstalkers to see your photos, know your friends, and read your blog—unless they're about what you do to cyberstalkers when you catch them.

➤ STEP #2: *Spread Disinformation*

Only post phony information about yourself. If you're tall, say you're short. If you live in Nevada, say you live in Nebraska. And if you are into defecation during sex, keep it to yourself . . . always.

The downside of this method is, of course, your friends on the Net won't know the *real* you. But isn't that the point of this whole stupid social networking shit anyhow?

➤ STEP #3: *Give up Your Computer*

Not only will this keep you safe from cyberstalkers, it might open up a whole new world to you outside cyberspace. While living without a computer and the Internet can seem daunting, it isn't. Make sure to check out "Your Connection Goes Down in the Middle of Warcraft" on page 217.

Now, what to do with that guy in the e-bushes?

How to Cyberstalk Someone

Let's say—just as a matter of interest, not because you wanted to hunt down your ninth grade crush who never called you back after prom—you want to cyberstalk someone. Let's call her Gregina Bergmina.

First, google her. Since she has such an uncommon name, you'll probably be able to find any mention of her. Beyond the simple search, you might be able to find her address and phone number on *whitepages.com*. You'll be able to see her friends, videos, and photos on Flickr, Facebook, and YouTube. (If you're really lucky, you'll be able to find homemade porn films on *YouPorn.com*.)

Now that you know all about her, set up a fake Facebook account and start flirting, gaining trust, and laying the foundation for a meeting, in which you can try to rape and murder poor Gregina Bergmina.

100. You Broke Your iPhone and Can't Afford to Buy a New One

At first, breaking it didn't bother you; it was just another gadget. Surely, in a few months there would be another new product and there'd be no need to replace your old iPhone. But now, everyone has one—except you. You feel like a freak; the only iPhone-less person in the Western World.

The WTF Approach to Getting a New F*#!-ing iPhone

▶ **OPTION #1:** *Save Your Money*

Cut down on food, stop going out, and skip some credit card payments. Do you want to be cool or not? Grow up and buy everything that everyone tells you that you need.

▶ **OPTION #2:** *Do It Old School*

Go out with your giant cell phone, old laptop, and Discman. You have 1,300 CDs, so you might as well use them. And for those of you who still have a cassette Walkman, even better. Just make sure not to mess up your Flock of Seagulls 'do when you're bobbing your head to *Purple Rain*. And if you really want to play up the retro thing to compensate for not having an iPhone, get really nutty and walk around with a boombox on your shoulder. Make sure it's as loud as it can be, so even people browsing the web and listening to music on their iPhone will be able to hear your tunes.

► **OPTION #3:** *Steal One*

Go to a local junior high in a wealthy town. One out of every three kids will have an iPhone. Even though in a poor neighborhood, it's one out of every two, focus your thieving energy on the rich kids. They're easier to beat up. Seeing a ton of bratty kids with the coveted iPhone will induce the anger you need to pull it off.

WTF ABOUT TOWN

After scouring junior high schools and grammar schools and eventually preschools, we found the youngest PDA owner in the country. His name is William "Billy" Schmidt. He's from Sioux Falls, Idaho. He's four. We sat down with the lad to ask him about his life in the fast lane:

WTF: Do you like your BlackBerry?

Billy: Yeah, I like it. It's red. Red is my favorite color. I like blue too.

WTF: Me too. I really like blue. So who got it for you, Billy?

Billy: My dad. He works a lot. He got me this so we could talk sometimes.

WTF: Which features do you use most often, Billy?

Billy: I like to make my daddy videos from my baseball games. I play right field . . . sometimes. This way he can see me play and not have to miss his meetings.

WTF: Do you think that it makes your life easier?

Billy: Uh huh.

WTF: That's great. Just one more question for you, Billy. While handheld communications devices like cell phones and BlackBerrys are incredible tools that allow people to connect in ways that have hitherto only been imagined, many social commentators warn that these technological advances also have a dark side: They force us to be constantly available, thus limiting our private lives. What is your take on the matter?

Billy: Hold on. I have a call . . .

Bonus WTF: Your Eight Year Old Won't Stop Throwing Tantrums Because He Wants a Cell Phone

Since when did an eight-year-old need a BlackBerry? Our kids have all become little phony Donald Trumps—and one colossal prick is enough, if you ask us.

The WTF Approach to Handling Your F*#!-ing Tech-Savvy Brat

➤ STEP #1: *Shoot Him Straight*

Tell him, "When I was your age, my favorite toy was an empty soup can and a stick. I used to hit the soup can with the stick, naturally. Now go outside and play—like a f*#!-ing kid."

➤ STEP #2: *Trick Him*

Buy a couple of paper cups, tie them together with a string, and tell your kid it's the latest gadget.

When the tech-savvy little rascal complains, tell him he's adopted. Then direct him to "You Find Out that You're Adopted" on page 134.

➤ STEP #3: *Get Him the Phone*

Hey, it's your fault for having a child in this day and age. Just like you *had* to have a Cabbage Patch Kid (or if you're a real young parent, Pokemon) back in ancient times, he wants to fit in, too.

101. Your Teenager Only Communicates in Text Message Lingo

You get this text from your daughter: OMG D, IDK Y R U POD? SRSLY. BRB FRL. W BFF. G2G. TTYL. 143.

And all you can think is: WTF? What do all these acronyms mean? Whatever happened to picking up a phone and calling someone? That's what you're paying the bill for! Your kid's texting has gotten *way* out of control. Every time you look at her, she's typing some silly message. It's f*#!-ing annoying.

If you find your teen turning into a text-crazed lunatic like so many PPL out there, take a look at how to handle it.

The WTF Approach to Your F*#!-ing Texting Teen

➤ STEP #1: *Make Her Call Someone*

Have her try talking to people for a change instead of typing messages. She might find out that they are not worth communicating with at all.

➤ STEP #2: *Break Her Thumbs*

It would be better if you could break all of her friends' thumbs, but that's impractical. So break hers. No one will expect her to text back.

➤ STEP #3: *Force Her into Texters Anonymous*

Here, she'll be able to talk about her problem with her fellow texters. With luck she won't pick up their loathsome habit of actually saying "LOL" when they think something is funny or "G2G" when they have to go.

PHONES OF THE FUTURE

God phone: The only phone that can connect you straight to the Lord himself. The Pope will pay top dollar for it.

Straight-to-a-live-operator phone: Tired of talking to robots?

Talk-to-the-dead phone: Check in with loved ones who have passed on.

Find-my-real-parents phone: Calls them so you can ask why they didn't love you enough to keep you.

➤ STEP #4: *Have Her Write Out the Rules to Text Etiquette 100 Times*

1. You cannot text more than once every thirty minutes if you're out with someone. If you do, don't expect him to ask you out again.

2. You must turn off the beep when you get text messages. That beep is annoying and you will be associated with that annoyance.

3. Don't send important information via text. If you're too lazy to call someone to pick you up from the airport, and instead text, "C U @ LAX 10AM K?" don't expect to be picked up. You need to put in a little more effort.

MATCH GAME

In order to keep up with your kid's constant texting, we've devised this test for you. Match the acronym with the meaning.

Acronym	Meaning
A) OMG	1. Obese man gut
	2. Oh my God
	3. On my gash
B) LOL	1. Laugh out loud
	2. Lick on the lamb
	3. Lions on lionesses
C) BRB	1. Bring Reagan back
	2. Big round balls
	3. Be right back
D) IDK	1. In the Dakotas
	2. I don't know
	3. Igloo dog Canada
E) GTG	1. Gone to Georgia
	2. Got to go
	3. Going to a gangbang
F) ASL	1. Age, sex, location
	2. Ass-sucking lips
	3. After-sex feeling of existential loss
G) BF	1. Big and fat
	2. Boyfriend
	3. Buttf*#!

Acronym	Meaning
H) GF	1. Gay fruit
	2. Girlfriend
	3. Get f*#!-ed
I) IMO	1. In my opinion
	2. In my orifice
	3. Inuit make me orgasm
J) JK	1. Junk
	2. Just kidding
	3. Jew Kid
K) MMB	1. My mom's big
	2. Make my bidet
	3. Mail me back
L) NM	1. No more
	2. Never mind
	3. Arizona
M) WTF?	1. Want to f*#!?
	2. What the f*#!?
	3. I have a giant cock.

Answers: A2, B1, C3, D2, E2, F1, G2, H2, I1, J2, K3, L2, M3

thanks and apologies

We would like to thank everyone at Adams Media, particularly Brendan O'Neill for his support of this project from day one. Special thanks to Deborah Warren, our wonderful and attractive agent.

We'd also like to take this opportunity to apologize to: Julius Caesar, Marcus Brutus, Attila the Hun, schmucks who talk at the movies, ugly hookers, hot hookers, the Swedes, unionized Hungarian whores, Julia Roberts, Richard Gere, ~~bouncers~~, Seamus the Irish bartender, Billy Joel, Bon Jovi, hick farmers, klutzes, Jack Daniel's, really drunk girls, Cesar Milan, Mothers Against Drunk Driving, ~~cops~~, nerds who drive us around while we're f*#!-ed up, doctors, widows, orphans, Barbra Streisand, Whoopi Goldberg, Hillary Clinton, Sarah Jessica Parker, Danish giants, Asian chicks, Europeans, Jews, waiters, Al Gore, old people, Coca Cola, ~~bosses~~, Spanish priests, porn addicts, grocery stores, pizza shops, fast food restaurants, ~~banks~~, New Jersey, Vancouver, the "Stans," slutty NGO chicks, computer salespeople, women, Mexicans, Jehovah's Witnesses, Californians, teenage girls, the Viet Cong, ~~yuppie scum~~, hillbillies, dead people, Gandhi, in-laws, Sidney Poitier, ~~telemarketers~~, James Mason, potheads, janitors, Angelina Jolie, homosexuals, Disney, Tori Spelling, Baron Hilton, ~~Paris Hilton~~, dogs, cats, teenage sluts, bald guys, Ron Jeremy, bloggers, America, ~~Nancy Reagan~~, Arabs, Boy Scouts, dwarves, Irish people, Jessica Biel, Lauren Conrad, Madonna, Fergie, Kathy Griffin, Janice Dickenson, Brooke Hogan, Heather Mills, Barbara Walters, Rosie O'Donnell, *Warcraft* players, ~~drug dealers~~, ~~Herpes Simplex 1~~, two-pump chumps, lion tamers, ~~cheating spouses~~, strippers, ~~meter maids~~, ~~panhandlers~~, Vietnam veterans, amputees, Chinese people, dry cleaners, ~~morons who work in fast food places~~, the handicapped, fat-asses, Elvis, smokers, ~~proselytizers~~, generous women with mommy complexes, ~~cyberstalkers~~, ~~chicks who take 1,000 pictures a night~~, ~~drug dealers~~, ~~priests who f*#!boys~~, ~~text messaging teens~~, ~~terrorists~~ . . . and ~~you~~.

about the authors

GREGORY BERGMAN is a writer and editor. He has received a B.A. in philosophy from Hunter College, and is the author of *The Little Book of Bathroom Philosophy*, *Isms*, and *Bizzwords*. He is married and has no interest in other women. We know, all the good guys are taken . . . WTF? He lives in Los Angeles, CA.

ANTHONY W. HADDAD is a writer and editor. He has received a B.A. in history from the University of California and an M.A. in international policy from the Monterey Institute. This is his first book. He resides in Austin TX.

For even more f*#!-ing fun, visit *www.WTFtheBook.com*